The Best is Yet to Come

MARC COLEMAN

BLACKHALL
Publishing

This book was typeset by Ark Imaging for

Blackhall Publishing
33 Carysfort Avenue
Blackrock
Co. Dublin
Ireland

e-mail: info@blackhallpublishing.com
www.blackhallpublishing.com

© Marc Coleman, 2007

ISBN: 978-1-84218-148-5 (HBK)
978-1-84218-142-3 (PBK)

A catalogue record for this book is available from the British Library.

Printed in Ireland by ColourBooks Ltd.

For Aoife

Acknowledgements

The most important person to thank is my wife Aoife who – so shortly after our marriage – put up with her husband becoming a stressed-out writer. Like any writer, I also owe thanks to my parents and grandparents for shaping my outlook and approach to writing. After this I must thank Derek Hughes for encouraging me to undertake the project. When that project finally got going, the staff at Blackhall Publishing – Elizabeth Brennan, Eileen O'Brien and Gerard O'Connor – were efficient, patient and supportive. My full-time employer Newstalk 106-108 fm – thanks to Denis O'Brien, Elaine Geraghty and Garrett Harte – helped to finalise the book, while George Hook was crucial in making the launch a success.

Guidance from T.K. Whitaker, Terry Prone, Michael O'Leary, Cormac Ó Gráda, Eunan King and Dan White was much appreciated. Gráinne Killeen squeezed a tight marketing campaign into an even tighter schedule for the book's production.

Thanks is also owed to Frances Ruane, Gillian Anderson, Alan Barrett and Edgar Morgenroth of the Economic and Social Research Institute (ESRI) for letting me squat in their library and ask them stupid questions, and also to Patrick Arnold for prompt and thorough research assistance. Neither the ESRI nor any of its staff should be associated with the opinions or conclusions I draw from ESRI research in this book. Thanks is also due to the ESRI canteen staff for their kindness as well as endless cups of tea. Colleagues in business and in the media have been very helpful in commenting on the book. Charlie McCreevy, Peter Sutherland and the Bank of Ireland between them contributed to a fantastic book launch.

Finally, I cannot thank, but I can commemorate the Irish Diaspora, which includes a large number of my family, for inspiring me to write this book.

A proportion of the royalties for this edition are going towards the Forgotten Irish Campaign.

Contents

Introduction

In one way, 1984 was a great year to be Irish. It may have been a year of high unemployment and emigration in Ireland; but it was also the year that saw Ronald Reagan, the grandson of a south Tipperary peasant, celebrate his re-election as president of the United States. Brian Mulroney – of vintage Irish stock – also celebrated his election as prime minister of Canada. On the other side of the world, Australian Finance Minister and future Prime Minister Paul Keating, and the Prime Minister of New Zealand Robert Muldoon were more cautious about their Irish ancestry, since it didn't go down too well with large sections of their voters. In 1984, Israel's prime minister was a Polish-born immigrant by the name of Yitzhak Shamir. Shamir had served as a resistance fighter during Israel's struggle to emerge as a state. Like other Israeli combatants, Shamir took inspiration from Ireland's struggle in the early 1920s, so much so that he chose the nickname Michael, after Michael Collins. There was something else Irish about Israel that year: Belfast-born Chaim Herzog, former student of Wesley College – and former Irish bantamweight boxing champion to boot – was its president.

As the descendants of Irish emigrants soared to new heights, the old country was sinking new depths. Poor and corrupt, the Irish Republic had nothing to offer its young in 1984 but unemployment. Continuing a century-and-a-half-old tradition, tens of thousands of young people were emigrating, most of them for good. Some thirteen years later, Ireland has become an economic success story, with one of the lowest unemployment rates in Europe and one of the highest rates of inward migration.

But is economic success also historical success? No historical experience can match the trauma of the Holocaust. But in a more moderate way, Ireland today is undergoing a similar experience to Israel in recent decades. The last fifteen years have seen economic expansion. But is that expansion an event in itself or a cause of something bigger? Is it an achievement to be praised, or the long-delayed occurrence of something that should have happened a century before? The fall in population that Ireland experienced during the famine of the 1840s was not unique; other countries experienced similar trauma in the nineteenth century, Finland being an example. But Finland's population recovered to pre-famine levels in little more than a generation. Over 160 years after the famine, Ireland's population is still only two-thirds of pre-famine levels. What possible relevance can this have for modern Ireland?

From just two million in 1948, Israel's population has grown to seven million people in just six decades. Refusing to accept the diktat of history, Israel has recovered its existence and language. The consequences for the displaced Palestinian people are severe and have to be noted, but are beyond the scope of this book. From a purely demographic point of view, Israel's growth is a remarkable benchmark for what Ireland might achieve.

Two years ago, as economics editor of the *Irish Times*, it was my job to report on the 2006 Census. In one generation, the Census reported, Ireland's population had risen by almost one-third. Since the turn of the new millennium – just six short years – it had risen by almost one-tenth.

To be sure, what is happening in Ireland is very different to what happened in Israel. Using emotional links that have endured for thousands of years, Israel's government brought its own Diaspora home. Ireland is creating a new home for the Diaspora of other lands. Having myself returned home – I worked in Germany between 1997 and 2004 – I was part of a tiny minority in a flood of hundreds of thousands of people, most of them with no ancestral ties to Ireland. Does this matter? Or does the bigger picture – the size rather than the composition of Ireland's population – matter more?

Ireland's Diaspora – some seventy million – is far greater than Israel's. The land masses of the Republic of Ireland and the island of Ireland are, respectively, three and four times greater than Israel's. For most of this seventy million, Ireland is not a place they long to go. Emotional ties between the land and its distant progeny are far weaker in Ireland than in Israel; but the number of those with Irish-born parents or grandparents is three million.

In December 2006, Peter Sutherland gave a speech at The Ireland Funds Christmas fundraising dinner. His achievement in becoming chairman of British Petroleum typified the other dimension to Ireland's emigration story. It is not just a story about the number of people our island has lost, but also about their abilities and talents. Launching the Fund to help those members of the Irish Diaspora who had fallen on hard times, Sutherland argued that it was time to bring the Diaspora home. He was referring to the poor Diaspora, the types epitomised in the 2007 film *Kings*. In that film, Irish emigrants in London toy with the idea of returning to the new booming Ireland, but never do. At the same time many hundreds of thousands with no such blood ties are not just thinking of coming here, they are doing it.

But wherever they come from, immigrants to Ireland are coming to a country the present population of which remains lower now than 160 years ago, when the population of the island was 8.1 million. Since then, Europe has trebled its population. The question begs asking: with a far more diverse economic base – and in an age of mass migration – what is Ireland's current population potential and what does it mean for our economy? Land size is not the only determinant of the answer; public governance, urban planning and economic productivity are others. When, in March of 2006, NCB Stockbrokers predicted that the country's population could reach six million by 2050, I published an article that same month comparing the population growth histories of Ireland and Israel.[1] I pointed out that – far from accommodating eight million – our state seems unable to cope with a population half as large.

Some years ago Tom Garvin wrote a book on why Ireland had remained poor for so long. The book was entitled *Preventing the Future*. In recent decades, globalisation and renewed confidence have finally allowed that future to be realized. The full extent of Ireland's potential is massive, particularly given the size of the Diaspora and of current world migration flows. As far as Ireland's growth is concerned, we are at the end of the beginning, not the beginning of the end. But if the Diaspora or other migrants come to Ireland, it will be to enjoy a future in which good housing is affordable and the quality of life is not destroyed by long commutes to work or an exorbitant cost of living.

Man does not live by bread alone. During The Ireland Funds Christmas dinner of 2006, the audience was told to 'look Irish but think Yiddish'. Along with the renewal of its people, Israel has restored the Hebrew language after centuries in which – in spoken form at least – it was dormant. In Ireland a debate is beginning about how continued immigration could threaten Ireland's identity and culture. Ironically, Israel's rapid growth and cultural regeneration was a process in which Chaim Herzog, an Irishman, played a close part, first as an independence fighter, then as a politician and eventually as president of Israel. If an Irish-born person can become a pillar of Israel's recovery then why can't immigrants with non-Irish backgrounds become more Irish than the Irish themselves, as previous immigrants did centuries before.

After the atrocities of the last century, the doctrine of racialism lies in disgrace. In the nineteenth century, racialism was a disturbing undercurrent of the post-famine experience of the Irish people. For both reasons, it has no place in any dialogue about the future of this country. Cultural purity is a different matter. As Israel did a half century ago, Ireland faces the challenge of restoring its cultural identity and national language and traditions. Far from being threatened by immigrants, the greatest threat to Ireland's cultural identity has always been the fecklessness of the native Irish. It was Israel's immigrants who turned a dying language into one spoken by five million people. Willing adopters, not destroyers, of their host country's

culture, most immigrants are mirrors on which a host country projects its images. Whether mass immigration strengthens or weakens
Irish culture will depend on how committed those of us here already
are to its survival. Economic improvement at the expense of cultural
emaciation is not progress. But if Ireland can match its stunning
economic achievements with a determination to retain its unique
identity, then this new century will witness the resurrection of one
of Europe's most ancient cultures.

PART I

DENSITY AND DESTINY

CHAPTER 1

Back to the Future

Absorbing these immigrants would have been beyond the ability of a well-established, prosperous country, let alone one newly born.

President of Israel Chaim Herzog, 1988

In 1935 Chaim Herzog emigrated from Ireland to Israel to take part in a struggle for the survival of his culture. Over a decade after Ireland's struggle under British rule had given her dominion status, Israel's fight for freedom was beginning. In land size and population Israel then was comparable to the province of Leinster. When it became independent in 1948, Israel was a country of some two million people. Despite some expansion in its territory since then, it is a land of only 20,000 square kilometres. By the time Herzog had become its president, Israel's population had grown to 4.1 million.[1] Less than six decades after independence, it now stands at just under seven million.[2]

A century ago it was put to the founder of Zionism Theodor Herzl that reconstituting a nation that had died two thousand years before was ridiculous. He replied, 'If you will it, it is no dream.' The impact of Israel's growth on the Palestinian people cannot be brushed away; but as an exercise in national recovery and reconstruction, Israel's recent history is impressive. Ireland's population remains below what it was in the mid-nineteenth century. Between 1850 and 1990, as Europe's population trebled, Ireland's was cut in half. But, in the last decade, Ireland's population, like a coiled spring, is rapidly bouncing back. Unshackled by economic inwardness and liberated by a globalised economy, Ireland is on a journey back to the future. From a peak population of 8.1 million in 1841 – some 6.5 million in the present day Republic – Ireland's population fell to 4.2 million in 1961, of which 2.9 million lived in the Republic. From that trough, the island's population has risen to just under 6 million and 4.2 million in the Republic. The last time Ireland's population was this large was in 1859.[3] Some time during our century, the population of the island will recover to pre-famine levels. It could also go significantly further. The data shown in Figure 1 carries a strong indication of a country undergoing a U-turn from failure and stunted growth. It's tempting to think that the black line hasn't finished its journey. When Ireland's population reached 8.1 million in 1841, Ireland was a net exporter of food. Even if the famine itself was unavoidable, and that is debatable, the population level prevailing at the end of it – over six million on the island – was a sustainable basis from which further growth should have developed. Now, Ireland's economy is well diversified and plugged into the world around it. The goal to recover the population levels of 1841 by the middle of this century is not just believable, but achievable.

LAND RICH, PEOPLE POOR

When relative land size is taken into account, Ireland's population just before the famine was broadly in line with England's. At around fourteen million, England's population was one and a half times that of the island of Ireland. Had our population grown at a similar rate to England's, twenty-seven million people would now inhabit the twenty-six counties of the Republic. The population of the entire island would be thirty-eight million.[4] Even by European standards, England was an early industrialiser. The congestion of its south-east corner gives another clue as to why England was always going to be a highly populated country. A short ferry ride from Europe's continental land mass has always made England part of Europe's economic

Figure 1:   Back to the Future

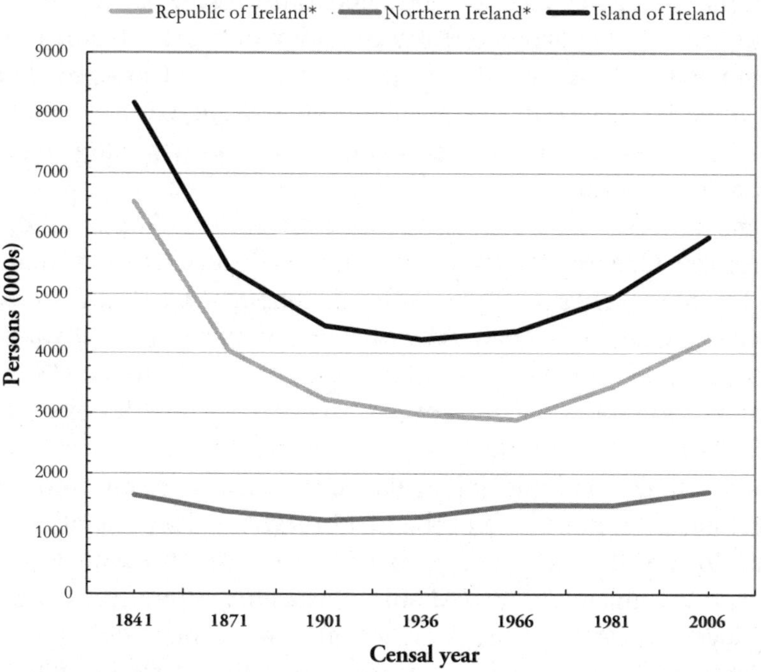

━━Republic of Ireland*   ━━Northern Ireland*   ━━Island of Ireland

*Before 1922 the geographical equivalent of

Source: Central Statistics Office, *Statistical Yearbook of Ireland 2006*; 2006 Census.

'core', spurring commerce and prosperity, and the growth in population that goes with them.

Even had the famine not touched Ireland, or even if it had but Ireland's population growth, like Finland's, rebounded quickly after it, Ireland would never have become as densely populated as England. But it would certainly have far more people than it has today.

With up to nine billion people set to inhabit the planet by 2050, Ireland enters the twenty-first century in a unique position as a rich, developed country. Ireland is also land rich. But it remains people poor. Situated on the temperate if rainy north-west fringe of Europe,

Ireland has one of the world's most fortunate locations. Western Europe's navigable location and temperate climate has led to a long history of trading and economic development, and has made it the most persistently successful economic zone in the world. Excluding the three Nordic countries that touch the Arctic Circle – Sweden, Norway and Finland – Ireland is the least densely populated country in Western Europe.

The Nordic country that doesn't touch the Arctic Circle is Denmark. Geographically luckier than Ireland, Denmark shares a land border with a big economic neighbour – Germany – and is close to another – Sweden. As globalisation makes these advantages less important, Ireland's advantages – good links with the US economy and low taxes – are growing stronger. Denmark consistently ranks as one of the world's most competitive, advanced economies; a country that has achieved a balance between economic and social development and between urban and rural life. Its population density, close to the EU average, is one that a country with Ireland's temperate climate can and should reasonably aspire to. At Danish population density levels, some 8.8 million people would now live in the Republic, over twice the current population. Some 12.5 million would live on the island. However, as Figure 2 demonstrates, as far as comparisons with other countries go, Ireland is on the lower end of the scale.

If comparisons with England and Israel are unrealistic, comparisons with Denmark could be argued as being conservative. Were Ireland to have Swiss or German population densities, the Republic would be home to anything between twelve and sixteen million people, while the whole island would accommodate between eighteen and twenty-four million. At the time of writing, the nation's ability to accommodate 4.2 million efficiently is being seriously questioned. Ireland is, according to some, already becoming over-populated. The argument is deeply flawed. Ireland is suffering from over-congestion, not overpopulation.

In the thirty-five years between 1970 and 2005, Malaysia's population grew by 234 per cent, Singapore's by 210 per cent and

Figure 2:   What if Ireland was as Densely Populated as…?

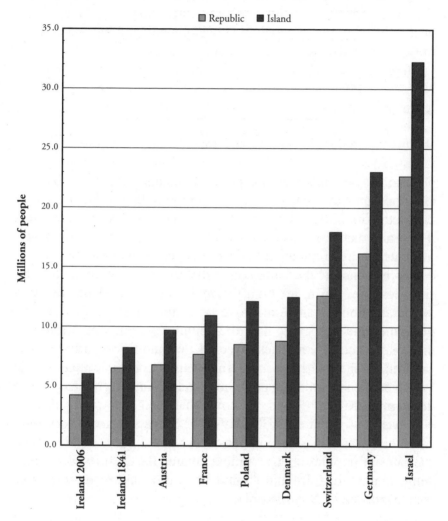

Source: Central Statistics Office, 2006 Census; UN Population Estimates 2002.[6]

South Korea's by 150 per cent.[5] Malaysia's population density has grown from 0.3 persons per hectare in 1970 to 0.8 persons per hectare in 2005, while South Korea's has grown from 3.2 to 4.8. Both have low populations by the standards of most developed economies, but

Figure 3: Population Density in Persons per Hectare

	1970	2005
Singapore	33.6	70
South Korea	3.2	4.8
Malaysia	0.3	0.8
Ireland	0.4	0.6

Source: United Nations, 2006.

are highly populated compared to Ireland's density of 0.6 per hectare. Denmark's density – 1.3 – is closer to that of Malaysia than to South Korea. But these countries are not considered congested. The reality is that poor urban and spatial planning has led to a situation where Ireland feels full, even though it is half empty.

Much economic literature argues that the more temperate a country's climate, the more highly populated it should be. Leading world economist and anti-poverty campaigner, Jeffrey Sachs, co-authored a study into how the geography and population density of particular countries affected their ability to improve the welfare of their citizens.[7] He found that tropical climates – in which Malaysia and Singapore are located – are highly adverse to economic growth.[8] Figure 3 shows that their geographical position hasn't stopped either Malaysia or Singapore from recording huge upwards shifts in population density. Figure 4 shows that the rates of population growth that created those shifts were stunning. If anything, Ireland should be able to house more people than Malaysia or South Korea.

GIVERS AND TAKERS

In the nineteenth century, Ireland was a giver of people to the world. The first wave of mass migration started in 1850 when the world contained just over one billion people. By the time it ended, mainly due to the outbreak of the First World War in 1914, some

Figure 4:   Rates of Population Growth 1970–2005

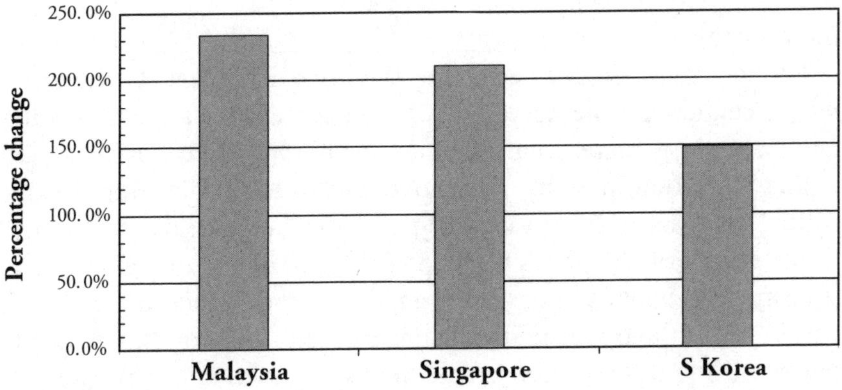

Source: United Nations, 2006.

55 million – about 5 per cent of the world's population – had changed their country of residence. Of that number, 4.5 million, or 8 per cent, were Irish. According to UN estimates, the percentage share of the world's population emigrating between 2005 and 2050 will be smaller than that between 1850 and 1914. But the sheer size of the increase in world population – the UN estimates an increase from 6.7 billion in 2006 to 9.2 billion by 2050,[9] an increase of 2.3 billion[10] – means that even if the percentage share is smaller, the total number of migrants between now and 2050 will number at least 100 million.

Even that number could be conservative. Migration has changed since the nineteenth century. Cheaper air travel has reduced barriers to movement. Faster and more powerful telecommunications have eliminated the need for migrants to sever ties with family and friends, reducing the social cost of migration. Most of the world's large cities are cosmopolitan places. Bangalore has Irish pubs; Dublin has Chinese welfare centres. Once emigration was a form of death: Irish emigrants were subject to a funeral-like wake on departure. Emigrating is now just like changing your hair colour, a convenient and reversible decision. Physically, psychologically and emotionally, people are more mobile than ever before. A culture of mass consumerism also means that the benefits of migration are more visible.

Globalisation should be having the opposite effect. In the nineteenth century people moved to where the wealth was. With capital and technology increasingly mobile, the big benefit of globalisation is that we should now be able move wealth to people. But globalisation has also affected the world's media. As well as the cultural implications of this, which Chapter 13 examines, globalisation is transmitting wants and desires around the world much faster than it can transmit the opportunities needed to realise them. Since people are unwilling to wait decades for their dreams to come true, higher emigration is the inevitable consequence.

Assuming a conservative figure of 100 million, if Ireland were to receive just half the percentage of what it contributed between 1850 and 1914 (8 per cent) between now and 2050, then four million people would come to our shores. That number has a symmetric quality to it: Ireland lost almost as many to emigration between 1850 and 1914. That's an annual inflow of over 90,000 people. However, the number is no less credible for being awesome or undesirable. One of the developed world's wealthiest nations, Ireland's GNI per capita is close to the top within the Organisation for Economic Co-operation and Development (OECD), and more than four times that of the poorest group member, Turkey.

HOMECOMING

Global migration is just one potential source of future Irish population growth, another powerful reason why net migration is likely to remain strong. After the first wave of migration, a million or more people left Ireland in the latter half of the twentieth century. Members of this latter million still alive, together with their children and grandchildren, are estimated to number some three million. If all of them were made entitled to an Irish passport and even one-third returned home between now and 2050, annual net immigration would rise by 20,000. When NCB Stockbrokers predicted in March 2006 that the population of the state could reach six million by 2050, they were on solid ground. In their study, entitled *2020 Vision*,[11] NCB examine a range of scenarios, the upper bound of which could see Ireland's population rise to as high as 9.5 million persons by 2050. Assuming that births exceed deaths by 20,000 per annum, this increase would require annual net migration to average at 75,000 persons. But, as noted above, a net migration figure of 90,000 is possible.

Assuming an annual net migration of 90,000, NCB's methodology would suggest that Ireland's population will top five million by 2013, six million by 2020 and ten million by 2050. From whatever angle Ireland's population is looked at – historically, in comparison to its peers, in the context of potential global migration, or in the context of the size of the Irish Diaspora – it looks very small indeed. However, on another scale was former President Mary Robinson's assertion – made during her inauguration speech in 1990 – that 'over seventy million people living on this globe claim Irish descent.'[12] But never mind seventy million. Never mind even seven million. At the turn of the twenty-first century, the Irish economy is struggling to accommodate 4.2 million people.

From whatever angle you look at it, a population of around nine million persons in the Republic and twelve million on the island is conceivable for Ireland by the year 2050. The opportunity – to restore what history took away – is a golden one. But although Ireland's population has grown hugely, any economy can grow by simply raising its population. Truly successful economies don't just grow their population levels, they also grow their productivity levels. And here is where Ireland has hit a bottleneck, a roadblock on the path of success. In 2006, Gross Domestic Product (GDP) increased in real terms by 5.6 per cent.[13] But the labour force grew by 4.6 per cent.[14] In per person terms, the benefits of recent growth have been negligible. Although highly educated, the new immigrant to Ireland is likely to work in a low productivity job, laying bricks, working behind shop counters or serving in hotels and restaurants,[15] like the typical Irish emigrant a century before. Rising costs and congestion are signs of an economy whose infrastructure and way of doing things has adapted to the needs of a small nation.

Although some migration from the Diaspora has occurred, the dwindling number is a sign that Ireland isn't big enough for the aspirations of both the Diaspora and those here already. Boomerang migrants – those whose time abroad was too short to sever social and cultural links with the home country – came back in their thousands during the 1990s. But, by the turn of the millennium, for a given sum of money, a second generation Irish-American could choose between a spacious condominium with a swimming pool in California or a semi-detached house in Ireland. By 2006, barely 5 per cent of immigrants were from the US or UK – the two countries where over 80 per cent of first generation Diaspora lived. According to the 2006 Census, only 18,174 of the non-Irish working in Ireland are of Irish descent. There are more Lithuanians than this and almost three times as many Poles.

As it becomes a costlier and more congested place, Ireland is less attractive to the Diaspora. Israel faces the same problem: congestion has brought its net migration rate to zero. In Israel's case the problem is unavoidable. With seven million people in an area that is one-third of Ireland's land mass, Israel is close to saturation. But in Ireland's case the problem is avoidable. We have the land. We have a network of global economic linkages – with the US, the Eurozone and, increasingly, China – that is unrivalled. We also have the dynamic of an economy that is still growing. What we lack is a will to exploit these things; a will to make the country work properly, to create a country where housing is affordable and life convenient. Regardless of the Diaspora, these are problems we have to solve anyway.

CHAPTER 2

Stunted Nation

That one million people should have died in what was then part of the richest and most powerful nation in the world is something that still causes pain as we reflect on it today.

UK Prime Minister Tony Blair, 1997

AN INCONVENIENT TRUTH

We are no longer, as Professor Gearoid Ó Tuathaigh puts it, the 'plucky victims of history'.[1] But Ireland's economic history is highly relevant to its future. Some argue that the past is a dangerous place. But economists and economic historians must analyse history. Other countries had famines. In 1866, Finland lost one-fifth of its population to famine – a similar share as Ireland twenty years before. But Finland's population soon bounced back. Hemmed in by the Arctic on its northern border and by negligent Russian masters on its eastern one, Finland was at a relative disadvantage to Ireland. But from having under half Ireland's population in the nineteenth century – and despite losing almost one-tenth of its population in a war against the Soviet Union – this remote country managed to surpass Ireland's population by the mid-twentieth century. As famine expert Cormac Ó Gráda and migration expert Kevin O'Rourke have documented, strong evidence exists that in most countries where it occurred, famine was followed by a rebound in population. Ireland was different. And if the reasons why Ireland was different were artificial, then they are reversible. And if they are reversible then no debate about our future is complete without them.

Ireland's famine was unique in that its demographic and economic impact lasted until within living memory today. Even by the standards of previous Irish depopulation episodes, this was traumatic. During the 1640s, a systematic military campaign by Oliver Cromwell reduced the population of Ireland by between one-fifth and one-quarter. A similar degree of depopulation had occurred in Germany at that time, because of the Thirty Years War. But within little more than a half century, the populations of both Ireland and Germany had recovered to levels prevailing before Cromwell's campaign.

So rapidly had Ireland's population recovered that the population of the twenty-six southern counties now comprising the Republic of Ireland was just over six million by 1841, six times the level estimated to have prevailed in the year 1600.[2] By 1841, Ireland's population density was level if not higher, than that of England – already one of Europe's most densely populated nations. Cromwell's reduction of the Irish population had been made good. In fact, evidence suggests that this had already happened by the year 1690.[3] But over a century and a half after the famine – three times that duration – the population of the Republic still remains below its 1841 level. Only in the six counties of Northern Ireland did populations surpass their pre-famine levels for the first time in 2002.[4] By contrast, according to the last UK census, England's population now stands at around fifty million.

What really damaged Ireland's population recovery after the famine was emigration. In a simulation exercise, Ó Gráda and O'Rourke calculate that – even allowing for the occurrence of famine – the population of the island of Ireland would have begun to recover in 1850 and would have reached ten million persons by 1910.[5] Even at this level, its population density would have been far lower than that of England.

Like the people of no other nation, except Israel, Ireland has suffered a devastating loss and scattering of population. Both countries have poured their essence into the world. In Ireland's case, the 140 years between 1845 and 1985 were a prolonged economic and demographic hemorrhage, interrupted only briefly in the late 1960s and early 1970s. Although Britain and Germany poured larger numbers into the sea of migrants, in Ireland migration was a much larger share of its original population.

In 1841, on the eve of the famine, Ireland and England were roughly equal in population density. But different economic structures – underpinned by different laws, different land owning structures and a great difference in the attitudes of government to their welfare – were soon to send these two nations in very disparate directions.

The fungus *Phytophthora infestans* – the potato blight – which arrived in Ireland in Autumn 1845, was the immediate cause of the famine. Having spread through the Netherlands, Belgium and the United Kingdom, the fungus had so far caused difficulty, but not disaster.[6] If Ireland had recovered from Cromwell's campaigns, it was now about to be devastated by one of his more enduring legacies. To more firmly plant the country in the hands of its colonial masters, Cromwell evicted Catholics – both native Irish and English – from their lands, leaving five-sixths of Irish land in the hands of a Protestant ascendancy. The native Catholic Irish, comprising four-fifths of the population, were left with the remainder, usually land of the worst quality.

Two generations later the foundations for future famine were strengthened when a series of laws known as the Penal Laws were passed, laws that were to have a profound impact on the country's economic structure during the eighteenth and nineteenth century. In full force by the early eighteenth century, these laws prevented Catholics from recovering their lost land by purchase, barred them from owning schools, bequeathing property and from taking leases.[7] Tenants were also required to pay two-thirds of the annual value of the land they held in rental payments to landlords, many

21

of whom resided in London.[8] Although they had eventually lapsed by the time the famine arrived, the impact of the Penal Laws left Ireland deprived of three elements crucial to economic success: an enterprising native business elite, a diverse base of economic activity and – above all, that vital ingredient – a culture of business and investment.

The mainstay of the economy was agriculture. Had it been productively organised, even this might have allowed Ireland to offset the impact of the famine. But insecurity of land tenure – together with continual subdivision of the land – stunted Ireland's only native economic advantage. Unable to own property, many Irish couples saw that having a large number of offspring was the only way to ensure financial security in the future. But with few alternative sources of income available, this led to the economically unviable practice of subdivision of land. As the population kept on growing and as the economy failed to diversify away from agriculture, the nation was heading towards a dead end. And for reasons discussed later in the book, this legacy of land division is still doing harm to the economy over 160 years later.

Although the implementation of the Penal Laws was less robust as the eighteenth century drew to a close, they had by then deprived the country of a commercialised and industrialised Catholic elite. Even allowing for these disadvantages, the pre-famine economy might have achieved some diversification but for distortions imposed on it by trade restrictions. The Woolen Acts of 1699 put a stiff duty on wool being exported from Ireland to England. A major Irish industry at the time, the duty was to seriously retard the development of large-scale wool production.

The contrast with Yorkshire, where duties were lower, is instructive. Yorkshire flourished, beating a path to that county's industrial prosperity in the nineteenth century. Then far smaller in population than Ireland, the population of the county of Yorkshire now exceeds that of the Republic of Ireland.[9] The contrast with the linen industry in the north-east of Ireland was also stark. Where wool – a largely Catholic industry – had been suppressed, linen – a largely Protestant one – had been actively encouraged as had manufactures that were protected by tariffs. A linen board had been established as early as 1711 and, by the nineteenth century, the industry had achieved a critical mass in the north-east of Ulster, where its progress was assisted by access to finance and an educated, confident business elite. The success of the linen industry in Ulster showed what might have been possible to achieve on the rest of the island had it not been deliberately held down.

It has been argued that Ireland's lack of natural resources – particularly a lack of coal and steel – was a factor behind the famine. As the steam engine replaced the water mill, large coal deposits gave Britain and Belgium a critical edge in the industrial revolution. But it was not an edge they retained. Ireland was capable of importing coal. Moreover, its significantly lower wages – adjusted for the cost of living wages in Ireland in the 1850s – were half English levels,[10] which would have offset most, if not all, of the transport costs involved. The success of industry in the largely coal-free north-east of the country also seems to undermine the thesis. Although it thrived in Antrim and around Belfast, in other parts of Ireland the textile industry could not achieve the scale of production needed to compete with England. In Connacht and south Ulster the collapse of the industry was to create many of the famine's future victims. The 1841 Census recorded that one in five working persons worked in the textile sector.

History and Theory

Modern economic growth theories differ about the precise causes of growth in developing nations. But there is agreement about its key drivers. The rate of savings is a crucial determinant of an economy's growth potential and – through this channel – its ability to sustain a growing population.[11] Most years between the passage of the Penal Laws and the famine were characterised by large current account surpluses.[12] Wealthy Irish residents were not undercapitalised. But many residents were only that in name. Landlords drawing rent from Ireland but residing in London, most of them with households there, had little incentive to invest in Irish industry. For most of the population, after rents had been paid to landlords and tithes had been paid to the Church of Ireland, there was nothing left for savings.

The Penal Laws and trade restrictions aside, but for one factor the Irish economy might have been able to generate an internal diversity sufficient to minimise the impact of the famine – education. After the Second World War, South Korea and Japan leap-frogged over their Latin American counterparts economically by investing in the education of their young. In the nineteenth century, the Irish were reasonably literate, but regular school attendance was probably confined to less than one in four children,[13] a legacy of Penal times, poverty and high fertility rates.

Before the famine struck, the result of all this for most of the country was well-nourished poverty. Foreign visitors to Ireland were as likely to remark on the good diet of the average Irish person as they were on the poor state of their housing and clothing. It has been estimated that Irish living standards then would be comparable to those of Ethiopia and Somalia today.[14] But Ethiopia and Somalia are surrounded by other poor countries; Ireland was then part of the richest empire in the world. It was rich in what were still the most crucial economic resources of the age – farmable land and fishable waters – and was in a strategically advantageous position between Europe and the emerging power of America. And yet it was a country of unemployment, poverty and malnourishment.

If there was a common source to all these problems, it was government. Modern economic theory is in broad agreement that the quality of institutions is hugely important to protect property rights and implement sound economic policy.[15] More than any other factor, this was what failed Ireland. Far from protecting them, the purpose of government in Ireland between the seventeenth and mid-nineteenth centuries was to enforce and uphold the theft of the only economic resource the native Irish had claim to – their land.

This was compounded by tariffs and restrictions on Irish exports that warped the evolution of Irish industrial development, geographically and in particular sectors. By the eighteenth century, Ireland began to develop a parliamentary democracy that – although confined to Protestants – might in time have fully represented the interests of the nation as a whole. The Act of Union 1801,[16] achieved through a combination of bribery and corruption, cut this short.

Only when the full force of the potato blight finally struck were the effects of this to be felt. Had it occurred fifty years before, a landed interest – albeit unrepresentative of the native Irish – would have acted to prevent the full magnitude of disaster that happened. In 1845, the year the blight struck, the government of the day – a Tory government under Robert Peel – was, by the standards of the time, relatively humane. In 1846, Peel's administration was replaced by a Whig[17] administration intrinsically hostile to the Catholic Irish. As far as many in this administration were concerned, the Irish deserved their fate.

Adopting a policy of *laissez-faire*,[18] the Whigs cut back the relief provisions established by Peel's administration. Influenced by Thomas Malthus, a prominent economist of the time, many Whigs – particularly the Whig Chancellor of the Exchequer Charles Wood – believed that Ireland was overpopulated and that the only correction for this was for nature to take its course.

In September 1848, Charles Trevelyan – permanent secretary of the Treasury – refused a request by the Chief Poor Law Commissioner Edward Twistleton for financial assistance for smallholders and cottiers in Ireland. Trevelyan noted that, if the Irish were instead encouraged to emigrate, 'we shall at last arrive at something like satisfactory settlement of the country.'[19] In other words, if mass emigration helped reduce Ireland to a state of political compliance, it was to be welcomed. *The Times* in London popularised the sentiment amongst the English electorate: 'In a few years more, the Celtic Irishman will be as rare in Connemara as is the Red Indian on the shores of the Manhattan.'[20] And if any doubt existed as to the real intentions of the government, the comments of leading Whig Lord Clarendon put an end to them: 'The departure of thousands of papist Celts must be a blessing to the country they quit.'[21] Two hundred years after Cromwell's armies landed in Ireland, the destruction of Ireland's population was repeated. But this time there was to be no recovery.

In some cases – Trevelyan's for example – the sentiments towards the Irish were based on misunderstanding rather than hostility. The popular writings of Thomas Malthus spread a genuine belief amongst the ruling elites that population growth lead to famine. By the end of the nineteenth century, Malthus' theories had been discredited. Technological advances were greatly increasing the food yield of land. From just under 266 million in 1850, Europe's population rose to almost 727 million by the end of the twentieth century.

But even had they been correct, Malthus' theories had no relevance to Ireland in the 1840s. A net exporter of food, Ireland's fundamental problem was that its population could not afford to buy food. Overreliance on the potato was the result. Compared to an average intake of 800 grams in Holland (and this was on the large side by European standards), the average daily intake of about one-third of the Irish population was between four and five kilogrammes. Of Ireland's 8.2 million population, 3.3 million were poorly paid labourers, while 1.4 were cottiers, the poorest of the poor.

A stunted political economy created a stunted economy which in turn created a stunted population. As people died or emigrated in their millions as a result of the famine, they left behind a falling population. Eventually, living standards rose as labour supply contracted and wages increased accordingly. But as *The Times* in London was to note, it was prosperity with hideous foundations.

Other European nations – even those like Italy where emigration had been significant – had achieved growth without starvation. Turning Jonathan Swift's parody of a century earlier – *A Modest Proposal*[22] – into grim reality, Ireland had achieved prosperity only by organising the death of a sufficient number of its own people.

Whatever happened between 1845 and 1957, it was not economic progress of any desirable kin.

POLICY PERMAFROST

By the year 1957 over a century had passed since the famine. But, in many respects, little had changed and, by the 1950s, the viability of the state was increasingly open to question. Having received a shock similar to the famine in relative terms, Europe was dusting itself down after the Second World War and rapidly achieving new heights of prosperity. At least eight million Western Europeans had died in the war along with almost thirty million Eastern Europeans. By 1945, Germany's economy had been knocked back to the year 1908.[23] The French economy had been knocked back to 1891 and the Dutch economy to 1912.[24] But by 1957 – as the populations of these nations rebounded – Ireland was still struggling to recover from the events of the preceding century.

On 25 March 1957 France, Germany, the Netherlands, Luxembourg, Belgium and Italy founded the European Economic Community (EEC). It was to copperfasten an economic recovery that was already in full swing. Between 1950 and 1958, Germany's economy grew by 7.8 per cent a year.[25] That of Italy grew by 4.0 per cent while the French and Dutch economies grew by 4.4 per cent and 4.3 per cent respectively. Locked in protectionism, Ireland was going backwards. In 1957, its Gross National Product (GNP)[26] – just 60 per cent of the EU average in per capita terms – had actually declined. In 1987 – some thirty years later – Ireland's GNP per capita was still 60 per cent of the EU average.

Hopeful developments were taking place in 1957. But they would take decades to come to full fruition. At the age of just thirty-nine, T.K. Whitaker became secretary of the Department of Finance the year before. He was appointed by then minister for finance, Fine Gael's reform-minded Gerard Sweetman. Whitaker was that rare breed in Ireland of the 1950s, someone with new ideas, and the Minister of

Industry and Commerce of the day, Seán Lemass, was determined to use them. With the political cover of Whitaker's endorsement, Lemass recommended a programme of reform to Cabinet in November 1957, a programme that would open up the economy to trade and foreign investment and eventually steer the state towards EU membership. As Whitaker himself recalls, the economic situation in the new state – still only thirty-five years old – was grim: 'The early 1950s was a period of permanent crises. It was all a series of disasters. There were no bright lights shining at the end of the tunnel. And there was an awfully depressed mood that was palpable.'[27] The major effect of the programme was to instill something that had been lacking in Ireland's economy since the 1840s: confidence.

The programme also broke the back of policy incompetence and policy inertia, although these were to make a strong comeback in the 1970s and 1980s. By the mid-1960s, for the first time in 120 years, Ireland's population began to increase. But it was a false dawn. Prosperity produced by liberalisation and the promotion of industry was cut short in the 1970s as a succession of unstable or minority governments tried to buy the electorate with favours, pushing up debt and taxes to crippling levels. In 1987 – from opposition benches – Alan Dukes' principled support for tough government cutbacks ended this vicious circle, but not before much damage was done.

During the 1970s and early- to mid-1980s, economic growth and employment became increasingly reliant on a build up of government debt. From being a quite small share of the economy in 1957, by 1987, exchequer debt had mushroomed to peak at 117.5 per cent GNP, a higher share than that of Sudan or famine-stricken Ethiopia. At 2.6 billion old Irish pounds, the cost of servicing that debt by then was equivalent to one-tenth of GNP. Net receipts from the EEC amounted to 4.2 per cent of GNP, helping to stave off disaster. But it could not go on. Economic growth ground to a halt in 1986 and, in the absence of drastic action, the future recovery of the economy was in serious doubt. Out of a labour force of 1.4 million, some 220,000 were out of work, an unemployment rate of over 15 per cent. The return to the net inward migration of the 1960s was to be cut short. By 1989, some 44,000 persons were leaving the country every year.

In 1987, Ireland was a more technologically advanced version of itself in 1957. And Ireland in 1957 was a land with less than half the population it had in 1847. In 2007, 160 years have passed since the famine. But only fifty years have passed since the opening up of the economy. And only twenty years have passed since the end of a disastrously incompetent approach to macroeconomic policies. In a very real and meaningful sense, the sense of competent economic policy formation, time had stood still for 140 years, or, if it had ever moved forward, those gains were quickly reversed. In economic terms, our population levels have only been able to start recovering from the famine over the last twenty years. In terms of its demographic and economic consequences, it's as if the famine ended only twenty years ago. We are now on the upswing of a prolonged recovery, a recovery with several decades to go – if we remove the roadblocks.

CHAPTER 3

The Density Dividend

COME AGAIN?

The little fields that cover the western seaboard are a reminder of the famine. But they are more than that. They are a symbol of a mentality; a mentality borne of a dysfunctional past that, unless we deal with it, will hold us back in the future. Attitudes to property, land use, planning, urbanisation and regional development have all been stunted by it. But for all its different dimensions, it has a common source: unique amongst the nations of Europe, if not the world, the Irish are unable to properly use space.

Looked at from a global and historical perspective, the idea of increasing Ireland's population by 90,000 people a year is feasible. But looked at from ground level in today's Ireland, it looks like madness. Overpriced houses, long commuting times and general congestion are entrenched in the public subconsciousness, as consequences of rising population. Economic output growth barely exceeds growth in the labour force. Economic productivity is growing weakly or not at all. Further population growth would produce economic growth. But in the absence of a crucial ingredient of economic success – the density dividend – it would not make the country better off in any meaningful way. Economic betterment is not just about making the national cake bigger. It is about making sure the size of the cake is expanding faster than the number of people eating it.

On one score at least, there is little doubt about the economy's potential to receive immigrants. By 2006, the number of houses being built each year, 90,000, was comparable to the number of immigrants entering the country. Between 1996 and 2006, 600,000 dwellings were built.[1] Some 266,000 were reported as being vacant on the day of the 2006 Census, of which 50,000 were holiday homes. Allowing for the fact that some occupants may have been absent that day, it still left around 200,000 empty houses in the state. The same Census reported that the average rate of occupancy in 2006 was 2.8 persons per dwelling.[2] In its central population forecast, NCB Stockbrokers predicted a rise in population of 1.8 million between 2006 and 2050. At first glance, vacant housing in Ireland can already accommodate almost one-third of that number[3] and – at recent rates of house building – the required accommodation for the remainder could be in place by 2026. Whether immigrants want to inhabit them and whether they can find jobs are two entirely different matters.

In 2007, far from encouraging more immigration, the Irish government announced that the right to work in Ireland – extended to all new Eastern European member states of the EU in 2004 – would not be extended to citizens of Romania or Bulgaria when they joined the EU. The reasons were more economic than cultural. Culturally, there has been little problem with immigration. Poles, Lithuanians and Latvians – the dominant immigrant nations – have blended in well, as have the many Chinese immigrants to Ireland. But with employment growth in construction and retail sectors coming to a halt at the time of writing, there are fewer and fewer jobs to attract immigrants. Has Ireland's short-lived status as a haven for economic migrants come to an end? And if Poles and Chinese can't find even low income jobs here, what possible chance is there of attracting immigrants from the Diaspora, those whose income and job quality demands are likely to be far more demanding?

THE DENSITY DIVIDEND

In 2006, NCB economists Eunan King and Dermot O'Brien hit upon the idea of the demographic dividend: the idea that, as Ireland's population rises, demand for a wide range of goods and services also rises, lifting economic output in the process.

Over the last number of decades, the ageing countries of Europe were seeing their labour forces decline as fewer Germans, French and Dutch had children. In Ireland the story is different. As the country's population rose from 3.4 million to 4.2 million between 1991 and 2006 – a rise of one-quarter – the number at work almost doubled from 1.1 to 2.1 million. The impact of this on the economy is huge and will continue to be so for decades to come. Making up a quarter of the population, households headed by thirty-five to fifty-four year olds decide half of the nation's spending. A tidal wave of demand is washing over the economy. From 1 million in 1996, the number of cars shot up to 1.6 million by 2004. Between 1996 and 2006, the number of annual housing completions doubled, from around 40,000 to over 80,000. With another two decades of high octane consumption to contribute to the economy, and being set to grow faster than any other age group in the population, this age cohort are pushing demand for goods and services to new heights.

This generation is also more educated than those that came before. Assuming this would continue, King and O'Brien predicted that the economy's productivity[4] would keep growing by 3 per cent until the year 2020.[5] Better education is certainly a prerequisite for productivity but no guarantor. At the turn of the millennium, it wasn't the lack of an educated workforce that held the country back, but a host of problems ranging from spatial strategy, urban planning, the cost of living and public services.

The standard of living is growing but, for many, the quality of life is falling. Competitiveness and economic productivity are also declining. Despite its unprecedented growth, there is something missing from the Irish economy. In addition to a temperate climate and coastal location, research by Jeffrey Sachs[6] found that there was one other critical quality that could greatly improve a country's economic potential: population density.

Population density is a subtle concept, but a powerful one. In terms of people per square kilometre, Sweden is one of the few countries in Europe with a lower population density than Ireland. But, from competitiveness to income per capita, it is one of the few countries that also regularly beats the Republic of Ireland in international measures of economic performance. This seems to contradict the idea that Ireland can benefit from a higher population density. But, as noted, population density is a subtle concept and is less about packing so many people into a square kilometre of land, and more about the combined effect of good spatial planning, efficient transport, proper urban planning and industrial clustering.

Its low population density aside, Sweden has one of the highest rates of urbanisation in Europe.[7] Organised into well-planned urban centres, eight million people enjoy efficient transport within and between cities and near universal broadband access, and the high social cohesion that these things bring.

In 2007, Danish Culture Minister of the time Brian Mikkelsen visited Dublin to apologise for the Viking invasions of 1,200 years ago. But when Viking armies from Sweden and Denmark came to our shores they established most of the towns we live in today. A thousand years ago they applied the idea that successive governments have so far failed to apply to policy making today: the density dividend.

The cost of that failure is rising. As long commutes test our patience and erode our quality of life, high house prices – caused fundamentally by low urban population densities – contaminate wage competitiveness and undermine the economy. Between 1996 and 2002, the average distance traveled to work nationally had risen from six to ten miles and from five to thirteen miles for rural communities, showing the underside of Ireland's economic growth. The trend stopped soon afterwards,[8] but only when the damage was already done. Because of poor urban planning, massive house building has not dampened house price growth – far from it. Over the same period, house prices have risen by

154 per cent nationally, by 136 per cent outside Dublin and by 201 per cent in Dublin.

In the summer of 2006, the American Chamber of Commerce – representing most of the crucial high technology sector – warned that the cost of Irish wages, driven by property prices, was causing many of its members to reconsider their activities in Ireland. In the following year, several high profile US companies, including Pfizer and Xerox, announced significant layoffs. And yet these companies drove the strong growth in GDP per capita – the so-called productivity miracle – during the 1990s and early 2000s.

Far from learning the lesson and densifying, the 2006 Census shows that Ireland is moving in the opposite direction. As the population of inner city areas, such as Dublin's Crumlin and Dún Laoghaire, falls, the populations in dormer towns far from Dublin City centre rise dramatically. Instead of being built densely in the centre of a city, apartments are springing up around the edge of the city, beyond decent public transport and in areas devoid of any possibilities to socialise without using a car. And that is just around Dublin. Instead of focused, clustered urban development around key cities like Dublin, Cork, Galway, Limerick and Sligo, Ireland is suffering the population equivalent of the measles; a messy proliferation of hundreds of small blotches describes its population growth.

As well as having the lowest population density in the EU outside Scandinavia, Ireland also has the third lowest share of population living in cities (60 per cent). And where other countries spread their urban population evenly between several large cities, Ireland suffers from chronic urban population inequality. One city, Dublin, holds one-quarter of the state's population and a half of its urban population. What is left is spread between population centres that most Europeans would have difficulty recognising as cities. Nominally, Dublin City had 506,211 inhabitants at the time of the 2006 Census. When its sprawling hinterland was added,[9] that rose to 1.2 million. With nominally just under 120,000 inhabitants, Cork – the second largest city in the Republic – was just one-fifth the size of Dublin.

Galway, Limerick and Waterford – the only other cities recognised as such in the Census – had populations of 72,414, 52,539 and 45,748 respectively. In other words, the metropolitan areas of Ireland's second, third, fourth and fifth cities, when put together, would still not exceed metropolitan Dublin.

The demographic dividend is conceivable. For it to become realistic, the density dividend has to come first. The principle is a simple, but powerful one: the larger the concentration of population, the richer the diversity of employment opportunities, the greater the ability to sub-divide labour into sophisticated tasks. And if there is one cornerstone of economic progress all over the world, this is it.

While the economy of a local village can sustain enough demand for a shopkeeper, a hairdresser, a pub owner and perhaps a butcher and a car mechanic, it cannot sustain jobs for computer programmers, design engineers or legal consultants. Cities can. And they can do more than that. The intercourse between people with diverse and complementary skills and perspectives is the elixir of economic growth.

When the diversity of economic activities hits a critical mass, we get what Adam Smith referred to as division of labour. Being able to concentrate solely on a well-defined range of work, workers find themselves able to produce a multiple of what they could before. Explaining the idea, Smith used the example of a pin factory where, instead of doing a little of each job, workers focused on one aspect of production: one on smelting the iron, the other on hammering it into shape, another sharpening it.

Cities large enough to sustain a rich diversity of worker types are more likely to sustain rich chains of activities that are both high value added and attractive to international markets.[10] As these interact in increasingly sophisticated ways, new markets are created. The computer software programmer meets the banker for whom she has been writing programmes, for social purposes. Together, they decide to go into business and market a product that multinational companies want. From being part of a local economy, the programmer's expertise and banker's knowledge of finance brings them into international markets. As Sean O'Riain has detailed, this is really happening in Dublin today.[11] But it is not happening in other parts of the country. As the failure of the aircraft leasing industry to take off in Shannon shows, critical mass and population density matter.

Ireland's industrial strategy is shifting away from attracting international manufacturing companies that create knowledge-based innovation. But achieving this requires technology spillover – the process of businesses learning technology from each other and applying it to their own products. In a globalised world, the more mobile people and technology are, the more important it is for cities to increase the quality of their workforces. Like a force of gravity, economic clusters attract high quality workers, enriching their attraction as a business location even more. But to do that, businesses need to be spatially confined in well-defined areas, that is they need to be located in decently sized cities.[12]

When it comes to locating large infrastructural investment, cities have another crucial advantage over towns, an advantage so important that economists have a special name for it: increasing returns to scale. As one of just many examples show, it's a concept that some in this country have serious difficulty understanding. In August 2002, the idea of a national stadium was discussed. The expense was considerable but in a large city like Dublin – if properly linked by urban transport – a national stadium could have paid for itself. If a sports event wasn't being held, a rock concert, a conference or a social function could take place to maximise both the financial and social return on the investment.

In a well-intentioned move, then Chairman of the Council for the West (a group that defends the perceived interests of the west of Ireland) Sean Hannick called for the government to put any stadium west of the Shannon. Athlone or Ballinasloe were suggested as possible venues with the following justification: 'It would take less time to travel [from Dublin] to the venues mentioned above than it takes to get from Bray, County Wicklow to Abbotstown, County

Dublin.'[13] If Hannick's comments had a point, it wasn't that a stadium needed to be built in the west. It was that urban transport between Bray and Abbotstown needed to be drastically improved.

Hannick provided a classic illustration of how we just don't get the density dividend idea. Ignoring Bray, even if Abbotstown's hinterland is restricted to the area of Fingal, South Dublin, Dún Laoghaire and Dublin City – it still has a catchment population of around 1.2 million people. The catchment population for Ballinasloe or Athlone is one quarter of this. Relative to its population, the west of Ireland is not badly served by infrastructure. But it is underpopulated and that in turn has retarded its economic viability and future. Instead of uniting to tackle that problem, hundreds of activist groups continue to lobby for state intervention to keep their local economies propped up on crutches, pulling the spatial structure of the economy apart as they do so.

The problem goes far beyond football stadia. Low population density raises the average cost of public transport; hinders the provision of hospitals, postal services, schools, proper broadband coverage, cost-efficient water supply services, and utilities generally;[14] deprives young people of employment opportunities in their own locality; leads to difficulty in sustaining local housing markets when a large local employer shuts down; and makes the maintenance of viable football teams problematic. Everywhere dysfunction lurks in modern Ireland, lying behind it is a story of underpopulation.

Huge though those consequences are when considered on their own, the consequences of this story go far beyond the provision of public services. In one of their comedy acts during the 1990s, the famous Irish comedy duo D'Unbelievables parodied the dominant character in the local village who happened to be the local butcher, the local pub owner and the local newsagent all at the same time. In the late 1990s, the jibe was no longer funny. Small populations within commuting distance of Dublin were growing in number. But with local populations too small to support more than one producer, the tyranny of the local monopolist was growing. Contrasting prices in Dublin with those outside Dublin in 2007, the Central Statistics Office (CSO) found that the price of a basket of goods was just 3 per cent higher in Dublin than in the rest of the country, a low differential given that prices outside the capital should be much lower. But average house prices in Dublin that year were 60 per cent higher.[15]

With higher densities, however, come larger markets of customers within easily commutable distances, bringing competition and lower prices in their wake. In 1995, Cathal Guiomard summed up Ireland's situation nicely: 'The great failing of the Irish market sector is the absence of sufficient competition. There are just two main retail banks, one very dominant newspaper group, one dominant beer producer, one beef baron, a dominant spirits manufacturer, a dominant video rental company, a dominant building materials firm.'[16] Many commentators are quick to assume a grisly conspiracy against the public. But much of this problem comes from the simple fact that Ireland's population is too small to support the kind of competition needed to drive prices down in the non-traded sector.[17] Likewise, Ireland's weak densification in rural areas is replicating the national problem for more localised markets.

Another consequence of Ireland's failure to reap the density dividend is the low productivity of its more recent growth rates. Despite an efficient construction sector,[18] building activity in Ireland is a low productivity affair,[19] where many workers are combined to produce relatively little value added. A US property developer can house at least a hundred people on a quarter acre. An Irish one would be hard pressed to squeeze in ten.

ONLY IN IRELAND

With over twice its land mass and one quarter of its population, Ireland has house prices that are significantly higher than Holland's. How is this so? With the vast majority of jobs being created in Dublin, Cork, Galway, Waterford and Limerick, the government is actively promoting increases in population in smaller towns outside those areas. This is happening before those smaller towns have been properly connected to cities by either road, rail or broadband. Although they should be spending their youth living in apartments near where they work and socialise, Ireland's up-and-coming generation has been banished to live in houses on the outer limits of cities, and often beyond, many miles from their place of work. Instead of becoming a teeming cluster of commerce, central Dublin remains a low density zone from which the 35- to 54-year olds – the crucial economic motor identified in the *2020 Vision* document – are increasingly banished by high prices and long commutes.

In 2002 the government announced: 'There must be a strategic expansion of rural villages and towns; people should be encouraged to live in rural areas.' Re-elected five years later[20] – in spite of rather than because of its record on spatial planning – the government hasn't changed its mantra. Instead of going back to the future, we seem bent on living in a feudal past.

PART II

DECADE OF DISTORTION

The influence of the public sector is the only question mark I would have about Ireland's future.

Eunan King, economist

CHAPTER 4

Red Bricks, Black Potatoes

History doesn't repeat itself. It just rhymes.   Mark Twain

AUGUST IS A WICKED MONTH

It has been said that those who fail to learn from the mistakes of history will repeat them. History doesn't repeat itself. But historical circumstance does, and it has a store of wisdom to offer anyone who wants to benefit from it. August 2005 saw the 160th anniversary of the potato blight reaching Ireland. A less serious but significant crisis was about to hit the Irish economy. It was a crisis we should have been able to walk away from without significant damage. If only action had been taken; if only lessons had been learned.

Since the early 1990s, house prices accelerated, mostly due to fundamentals: population had risen rapidly and interest rates had shifted down to historic lows, pushing annual house price growth to double-digit rates. But, by 2005, house price inflation had moderated to a more sustainable 5 per cent. At a confidential meeting with Ireland's Central Bank, officials of the Organisation for Economic Co-operation and Development (OECD), an organisation with a deep knowledge of Ireland's economy, warned that Irish house prices were overvalued by around 15 per cent. The Central Bank's refusal to comment when news of the meeting was leaked was interpreted as silent agreement with what the OECD was saying.[1] The figure was far less than some apocalyptic estimates (some with 40 per cent overvaluation). Far from signaling an imminent crash, this level of overvaluation could be dealt with if the right policies were pursued. Restraining borrowing growth and tackling land supply and planning bottlenecks could have kept house price growth below income increases for a few years, enough time for overvaluation to unwind.

In other words, the news was not a huge problem. But what happened next was. Right under the Central Bank's nose, the exact opposite of the policies needed were about to be implemented. From a manageable 5 per cent, house price inflation was about to take off. With the supply of building land in desired city and town centre locations severely limited, a tide of credit was about to wash over the economy. Mortgage providers increased the maximum term of loans from between twenty-five and thirty years to forty years. Over the course of 2005 and 2006, banks desperate for business in a more competitive market scrambled to offer 100 per cent mortgages to young borrowers, who were about to buy houses that were overvalued. The sums that banks would advance to borrowers went up from around three or four multiples of income to five or six.[2] Ireland was about to prove one of the most repeated rules in economics: that inflation is always and everywhere a monetary phenomenon. As borrowers were allowed to spread the burden of repayments over four decades, they were robbing their old age to pay for inflated house prices.

From already high rates, private sector credit rocketed. Borrowing for real estate activity rose by €20 billion between June 2005 and June 2006, a whopping increase of 65 per cent in a twelve month period.[3] Having risen threefold between 1996 and 2005 – and just when they needed to grow at a settled rate of around 5 per cent – house prices jumped up by a further 15 per cent in just one year. If they were 15 per cent overvalued in the autumn of 2005, they were around 25 per cent overvalued by 2007.[4]

PARALLELS WITH HISTORY

In 2007, the Bank of Ireland reported that we are the second wealthiest nation in the world.[5] On the face of it, we don't need to worry. But Ireland is also the second most indebted nation in Europe after Holland.[6] The comparison with the Netherlands is instructive. Both countries were hit by the potato blight in 1845. But, where the average poor Dutchman's diet was well diversified and contained less than half a kilogramme of potatoes per day, the average Irishman's contained four times that amount.

Like their farmers' diets a century before, the Dutch have a well-diversified asset base. Shares, international government stock and other assets are testaments to the age and richness of that country's economy, an economy that has been central to the European economy for four hundred years. As of 2007, the vast bulk of Ireland's wealth – around 70 per cent – is held in residential property.

The share of the population who were landless workers, already staggeringly high before the famine, rose as the 1830s and 1840s wore on. In 1824, tariffs on manufacturing goods – one of the few sops to the domestic economy – were abandoned. Denied the stimulus of international competition and without the human expertise or capital to become viable, the manufacturing sector became weak and uncompetitive. As it collapsed, reliance on agriculture increased and the Irish economy headed into the 1840s in an increasingly lopsided condition. In short, the Irish economy had a productivity crisis.

Fast-forwarding by over a century and a half, a productivity crisis – with far milder consequences – is now being caused by overdependence on one sector of the economy: property. Having grown in real terms by 6 per cent, the performance of the Irish economy in 2006 was impressive. But with the number of workers rising by 5 per cent, growth of this magnitude was almost inevitable. In per person terms – the only terms that matter – the economy was barely growing at all.

Of the 166,000 new jobs created between February 2005 and February 2007, 108,500 had been created in the private sector, but,

**Figure 5: Year-on-Year Growth of Domestic Demand
and External Demand**

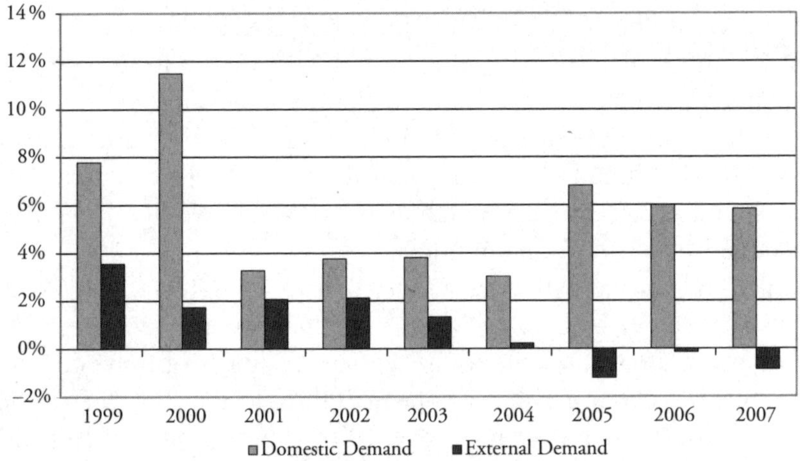

Domestic Demand   External Demand

Source: Central Statistics Office 2007.

of this, 49,000 – almost half – were in construction. A further one-fifth were in the retail sector and almost one-fifth were in the financial services sector. In other words, almost all jobs created in the last two years of the so-called Celtic Tiger were in the non-traded sector. It stands to reason. In that period the external economy – exports and imports – contributed negatively to the economy as debt-fuelled import growth exceeded export growth, a trend that has been intensifying since the turn of the decade (see Figure 5).

In 2005, the economy's exposure to property was significant. But it was also easily manageable. But, by 2007, the credit surge made the problem more serious. The construction industry employs one in seven of the workforce, double the EU average. From a peak of 280,000[7] employed in the construction industry, some 140,000 stand to lose their jobs as output and employment shares return to EU norms. Directly, construction accounted for over 17 per cent[8] of GDP in 2006, double the share recorded in 1988.[9] Indirectly, the share of construction and property market activity in GDP was estimated at anything between one-fifth and one-quarter. By that year, one-fifth of tax revenue levels were being generated by tax revenues indirectly dependent on these sectors. But even the share of the tax level understated the dependence on growth in those revenues. By 2006, over half of that growth – essential to finance rapid increases in government spending – was dependent on either the property market or the construction industry.[10]

The parallel with history has two more dimensions worth noting. The first concerns regional disparity. In the nineteenth century, dependence on the potato was highest in the western regions of the country. Today, the skewed nature of economic development outside Dublin has left Ireland's regions over-dependent on the construction and agricultural sectors. At the time of writing, the construction sector is undergoing a decline in output and employment while agriculture is undergoing a more long-term decline. Dr Ronnie O'Toole[11] has estimated that around two-fifths of employment in regional areas of Ireland depend on these two sectors. By contrast, Dublin now accounts for over one-third of foreign-owned – the most high technology employment – jobs in the country. Despite strong efforts by central government to encourage them away from Dublin, the capital exerts a gravitational pull on foreign direct investment (FDI) by virtue of its size. Border areas, by contrast, have seen their share of aggregate employment decline in recent years.

The second is the revival of one of the most despised characters of the nineteenth century, a prominent and possibly more potent force in our economy today: the gombeen man. The gombeen man was employed by a landlord as a rent collecting agent and was allowed to extract additional charges from the tenants at his discretion. Economists refer to these charges as 'economic rents', a term also used to describe the actions of monopolies. In Ireland today, many existing home buyers – newly weds or couples with growing families – are trying to trade up, but the state stands between them and their object. Stamp duty, ranging from anything between 3 and 9 per cent, and with average house prices for second-time buyers averaging €337,000 in July 2007, requires these buyers to give the government in the region of €10,000 simply for the privilege of buying a home. The failure to keep the thresholds for higher rates of stamp duty in line with rapid house price growth has left some families – particularly in Dublin where property prices are among the highest in the world – with bills of €50,000 or higher.

Like the gombeen man's fee, the effects of stamp duty go beyond its inequity. Between the middle of 2005 and 2007, the European Central Bank (ECB)[12] raised its key interest rate by two percentage points. Accordingly, house price growth began slowing in early 2007. By the summer of that year the main index of house prices, the Permanent tsb/ESRI Index, suggested prices were falling by modest single digits. But that index lagged behind events in the market by several months and, by autumn, prices in some parts of the country were falling by up to 20 per cent.

To most people, a fall in house prices was acceptable, even welcome. But something worse than this was happening. In May, figures published by the Irish Bankers Federation (IBF) showed how – in the first quarter of 2007 alone – new mortgage lending was 19.1 per cent lower than a year before.[13] Interest rates were lowering prices, which was natural. But stamp duty was killing activity, strangling the volume of trading in the housing market. Employment in the construction industry was also falling, at an increasing rate. The CSO Index of Employment in Construction went from registering modest single digit growth in January, to zero growth in the spring, to registering declines of 1 and 2 per cent in June and July respectively. By then, the government was also suffering as revenues from stamp duty, capital gains tax and capital acquisitions tax began falling significantly below target.

We could echo the words of John Mitchel, a leader of the Irish independence movement in the 1840s, who wrote that the Almighty may have sent the potato blight, but the English government sent the famine. Falls in house prices had certainly been caused by ECB interest rate rises. But the government's role in the economic slowdown – allowing credit and government spending to rise too rapidly in 2005 and then overtaxing the property market in 2007 – cannot be ignored. As Mark Twain said, history doesn't repeat itself, but it does rhyme. Some 160 years on and the British are gone, proving that we don't need them meddling in our economic affairs. We are quite capable of messing things up on our own.

By 2002, the economy was in a position of broad balance. At 2.8 per cent, the quality of growth in GNP justified the modest quantity of it. Exports – the mainstay of economic growth up until that period – were growing by a healthy 4.5 per cent, ahead of import growth. Personal consumption was growing by a lesser but still healthy 3.8 per cent. Manufacturing employment made up one-seventh of the workforce. Construction employment accounted for one-tenth, above the EU norm of 7 per cent, but by an acceptable margin given the country's young population. The next five years were to drastically warp the economy. Strong growth rates continued but a growing number of people found that their livelihoods depended on activity levels that, under current conditions, were unsustainable.

A Pause for Reflection

This is not the nineteenth century. Today, Ireland's economy is able to sustain a far higher population of well-off workers than it was in 1841. The 8.2 million that inhabited the island in 1841 could, with a less warped economy, have been sustainable. Although too many relied on the potato, the country was a net exporter of food. A distorted and lopsided economy produced a disaster that never needed to happen. Chapter 2 noted how, even allowing for famine deaths, a different policy response would have given rise to an all-island population of ten million by the end of the nineteenth century. Since the mid-nineteenth century, the population of Europe has almost doubled. To imagine that Ireland could reach a population of nine million – barely more than pre-famine levels – over two hundred years after the famine is hardly fanciful.

But the economy has run into a cul de sac. Although economic growth inevitably follows from population growth, overreliance on the property market and the construction industry, excessive credit and falling competitiveness do more than affect the ability to turn that into growth and well-being per person. They also challenge the social and political viability of the idea. For these reasons, rebalancing the economy is a matter of national priority if we are to accommodate the population growth that can and should happen. Building houses in Ireland isn't the problem. The problem is that the houses we have are too scattered and poorly connected by infrastructure. This is also a sign of an overhang of property activity; an overhang waiting for a hangover. Connecting these houses to areas of high employment with transport and broadband, building more houses in high employment areas, densifying population by improving spatial strategy and land use – all topics dealt with in later chapters – are the main components of a challenge that will take decades to realize. By the start of 2007, there was enough spare housing to accommodate another 600,000 new citizens. Some conclusions are possible: if we are preparing for when the Diaspora come, we are making a damn good start; if we aren't, we're in deep trouble.

At the time of writing, latest forecasts from the ESRI indicate that the so-called Celtic Tiger would expire in 2008. From a peak of around 80,000 houses in 2007, housing construction will fall to 65,000 in 2008.[14] Employment will rise by 50,000 in 2007 (compared to an impressive 87,000 in 2006), and by just 12,000 in 2008. Most interestingly, it predicts that net migration – the mainstay of recent population growth – will fall from 70,000 in 2007 to barely one-third of that, 25,000, in 2008. Is the dream over? What if – in fact – there was no Celtic Tiger? What if recent economic trends are not the beginning of the end. What if they are just the end of the beginning?

Ireland's future has not been prevented, merely delayed. In the early 1990s, it finally began to happen. The day before the ESRI predicted the end of the phase of growth known as the Celtic Tiger, startling evidence emerged that Ireland's process of historical recovery was just pausing for breath. In the second quarter of 2007, as house prices were beginning to fall, planning permissions for new houses and apartments jumped by 21 per cent year-on-year. Although accepting the need for a correction in the short-term, the building industry is far more optimistic about longer-term demand growth than most. The share of employment in construction is too high. But if employment in the economy overall can grow quickly, then that share can fall to sustainable levels without any drastic reduction in the level of construction employment. To do that, the economy must now ascend to a far higher level of productivity, a level that is indigenously rather than multinationally driven. That productivity will be the foundation on which the nation's full potential can be built.

CHAPTER 5

Bribes for Tribes

The quarrels of petty chieftains divide them ... rarely will two tribes confer to repulse a common danger.

Roman historian Tacitus' comment on
why Rome conquered the Celts

2002: AN IMPORTANT ANNIVERSARY

In the year 1002 Brian Boru, king of Munster, conquered the last tribe resisting his rule in Ireland. This was to be the first and the last time a truly independent force ruled over the entire island. Had his rule survived, an Irish state might have emerged, an entity with its own laws to guide its commerce and social intercourse and an army to protect the country and its culture from invasion. But Ireland's history is famous for its tribalism. Boru would have ruled Ireland but for the tribes of Leinster. One hundred and fifty-five years after his death, a tribal feud led to the Norman conquest of the country in the twelfth century. Four hundred years later – and but for each other – the Ormonds or the FitzGeralds might have ousted their English heirs. Today, in the twenty-first century, the people might be ruling, but for tribal interests that seem to control every aspect of government policy.

But a thousand years after Boru's triumph, something hopeful was happening. In 2002 Bertie Ahern had just been re-elected as Taoiseach and, for the first time, had command of a majority in the

Dáil. Moreover, it was a majority government with a broad ideological cohesion. Except for the previous Fianna Fáil[1]-Progressive Democrat coalition between 1989 and 1992, previous coalitions had involved tension between conservative or centrist parties and the Left. Composed of the same parties, the preceding government relied on four independent TDs to sustain a wafer thin majority. Influential and charismatic, the independent Fianna Fáil TD for Kerry South, Jackie Healy-Rae, symbolised the relationship between government and local interests. Between 1997 and 2002, millions of euro went into road building in Healy-Rae's Kerry South constituency, an area that badly needed it. But the way in which – and the reasons for which – that beautiful county was given priority begged questions, at a time when there was no proper motorway linking any two Irish towns.

But this wasn't just a Kerry phenomenon. It wasn't even geographical. Every five years or so, in the year before an election, local and sectoral interests across the country exploit the largesse of government, some deservedly, some less so. As Chapter 11 explains, Ireland's sensitive electoral system means that, instead of spending by the nation and for the nation, governments of all hues are often forced into sporadic and fragmented bribery that destroys long-term cohesive planning and stunts the cycle of government spending. Part of the distorted growth story covered in the last chapter was caused by the fact that, in the two years leading up to the 2007 election, government spending had risen by 25 per cent. Ireland is a land of bribes and tribes; a land where you bribe some of the tribes all of the time and all of the tribes some of the time. In 1002 Brian Boru had forced the tribes to kneel and pay tribute. In the election year of 2002 and five years later in 2007, and every election year beforehand, it has been the government that knelt and paid tribute to the tribes. As shown in Figure 6, the phenomenon is evident from the rates of increase in government in the year before an election.[2]

Independent of independents, in 2002 there was some hope that the government was now free at last to rule for the nation. There

Figure 6: Rate of Increase in Government Spending 2000–2007

2000	200 1	2002 election	2003	2004	200 5	2006	2007 election

Source: Department of Finance, Budgetary and Economic Statistics, 2007; Stability Programme 2007.

was much to do. The population was over-concentrated in the eastern half of the country. In spite of rather than because of prosperity, congestion was growing (a consequence of bad planning). House prices were chronically high.

As far as the first problem was concerned, action was being planned. Some thirty-five years after it was told do so,[3] the government attempted to deal with the eastern bias of the country's population growth. Due to be finalised that year, the National Spatial Strategy was expected to achieve a more efficient and balanced spread of population across the country. Linked with but separate from the Strategy, the government's policy of decentralising the public service was being worked on. If well planned and focused, this had the opportunity to complement the Spatial Strategy and improve the efficiency of the public sector. But as well as changing where the public sector was located, the government also needed to change the way it worked. Nominally low by international levels, Ireland's tax levels were on a par with tax and spending in countries of the EU like France and Germany, when several factors were accounted for.[4] Total government spending on public services had risen by 220 per cent in the ten years to 2002. But having changed little since the foundation of the state, the public sector was delivering poor results. The Public Service Benchmarking Report, due in that year, was expected to start solving the problem by increasing public sector pay in return for public sector trade unions accepting serious reforms.

Yes, a thousand years after the situation last existed, it seemed that 2002 might just be the year when the higher interests of the nation would finally take precedence over those of the tribes. It was not to be.

GO EAST, YOUNG MAN

Building viable economic communities and sustaining a high standard of living are two rewards of the density dividend. But, no matter how obvious the benefits, the idea of living in cities seems distinctly un-Irish. It was left to Viking invaders to establish Ireland's first cities in the ninth century. A thousand years later, the National Spatial Strategy set out a second attempt.

Aiming to create 'a more balanced regional development' by moving population growth away from Leinster, it was also hoped that the initiative would concentrate Ireland's urban population more efficiently. It was to fail on both counts. Of the 319,000 increase in the state's population between 2002 and 2006, two-thirds, 190,000, occurred in Leinster. 'Leinsterisation' seems to have been official government policy for generations, but is in fact the result of powerful regional and sectoral forces. Unfortunately, the government's weak and uncoordinated attempts to counter them haven't worked.

Having 30 per cent of the population of the twenty-six counties in 1841, Leinster's population was broadly in line with that of its land mass.[5] By 2006, Leinster contained 2.3 million people, over half the state's population. Although the population of the state has risen to two-thirds of what it was in 1841, the population of Connacht and Ulster combined is just one-third of that benchmark (see Figure 7).

Within Leinster, Dublin City continues to grow slowly as the population grows strongly. But instead of other towns on the west

Figure 7:   The Leinsterisation of Ireland

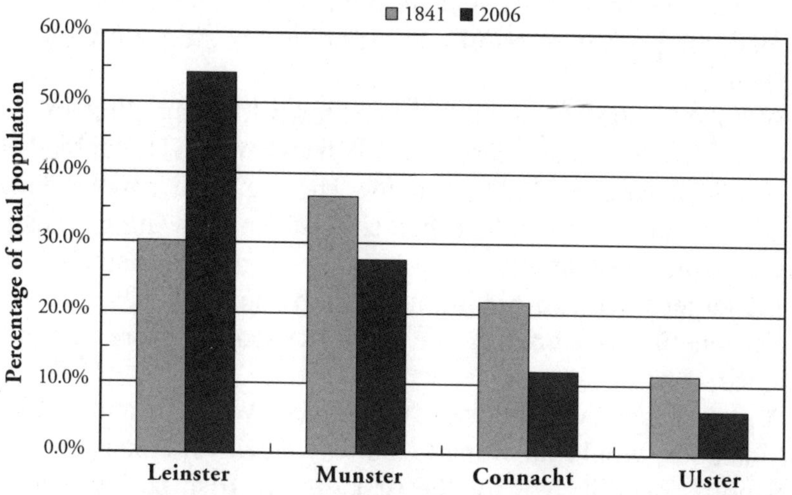

Source: Central Statistics Office Statistical Yearbook 2006; 2006 Census.

or south coast growing, counties around Dublin are being swallowed up by the capital. Refugees from Dublin's expensive housing market, many tens of thousands of people in Leinster now commute unwillingly to work in a city where they would rather live.[6] Growth in Kildare, Meath, Louth and Offaly has been rapid. Beyond the Pale, only Galway City has seen strong growth. In other regional towns growth has been disappointingly low and, in some cases, negative. The net shift that needed to occur hasn't. As Ireland continues being Leinsterised, Leinster continues to be 'Dublinised' in the sense of it becoming an extension of the capital.

The crucial challenge of the Spatial Strategy was to create one – if possible two or three – rivals to Dublin City. As noted above, it is not the low number of towns in Ireland that is the problem, but the inequality of their size. With little comprehensible logic, multi-centre gateway towns ('hubs') were identified with little prospect of rivaling Dublin. Instead of focusing on Cork, Galway and Limerick, towns like Athlone, Mullingar, Tullamore, Killarney and

Tralee were included. The Strategy document targeted future population levels for a 'city and its hinterland'. The crucial insight needed, the priority to build real cities, was missed. How did this happen?

Worried by the exclusion of 'their' town from the Strategy, and any negative political consequences, backbench TDs lobbied the government hard as 2002 went by. The idea that smaller towns would actually benefit rather than suffer from allowing the nearest city to grow substantially – that by creating more sustainable jobs in the larger town and linking it to nearby smaller ones, everyone could benefit – was unthinkable. With transport networks so undeveloped, it wasn't hard to see why.

A proper motorway between the likes of Westport and Galway, for instance, would have made Galway's growth consistent with Westport's benefit. Not for the first time in Irish policy making, carts were put before horses. The proper implementation of the infrastructural investment comes after a Spatial Strategy that it should have preceded. There were other anomalies. Dundalk was included in the list of hubs; Drogheda was not, a clear sign that government policy was becoming a victory of lobbying over logic.

Densely packed populations are more likely to be economically viable, while sparsely spread populations are less likely to be viable. Statistics on viability prove that Ireland is no exception. They also challenge some deeply held regional prejudices. Traditionally, Dubliners like to portray Cork men as types who would steal your eyeballs, sell them back to you and run off with your wife. In 2007, the CSO had news for them. On the contrary, Cork and Kerry are making the largest relative contribution to the wealth of the nation. Comprising what the CSO terms the 'South West' region, the gross value added (GVA) per person – a measure of their average economic output – was 22.3 per cent higher in these counties than the national average in 2003.[7] But disposable incomes, again on a per person basis, were 2.6 per cent *lower.* However much the presence of heavy-hitting multinationals – Pfizer for example – might distort the figures, they prove that Cork and Kerry are, in economic terms, givers rather than takers.

For Dublin and its three neighbouring commuter counties of Kildare, Meath and Wicklow, the situation is similar but less generous. The GVA per person in this area was 16.8 per cent higher than the national average in 2003. The disposable income per person was 8 per cent higher,[8] implying a lower net transfer to the rest of the country. Put together in the midlands region, the counties of Laois, Longford, Offaly and Westmeath have the lowest GVA per person of all the regions in the study. But the region's disposable income was 93.2 per cent of the national average. At least the figures show that regional redistribution is working. But is this going to be a permanent state of affairs, or is something going to be done to put the midlands on its own feet economically?

The midlands suffers from distance from the coast, accentuated by a lack of motorway access to the country's largest towns. Its largest town, Athlone, has less than 20,000 people in its immediate environs, but is in a strategically advantageous position slap-bang in the middle of the country. A strategy for increasing the region's economic productivity – real economic productivity – might have focused on that important fact by designating a Galway-Athlone-Dublin axis and locating as much international investment as possible half-way along it. Instead, government efforts at helping the region are wasted on perhaps the most misconceived policy initiative in over two decades – decentralisation.

DECENTRALISATION

Describing decentralisation as a 'plan' is flattering. The underlying intention – moving economic activity into the regions – is laudable. But what the government is trying to move is not exactly economic activity. A typical example is the attempt – still ongoing at the time of writing – to move the state employment and training agency FÁS from Dublin's Baggot Street to Birr in County Offaly.

Marketed as greatly improving the quality of life for public servants involved, for some of them decentralisation is just that. A handsome town set in fine scenery, Birr is near mountains and boasts amongst the lowest house prices in Ireland. What the government does not understand is that, although it is vital to move economic activity to the regions, this has to be an organic process. Like Stalin's attempt to make rivers run backwards, decentralisation is bringing policy implementation activities to small towns that benefit little from them. State-owned activity is low rather than high technology and bureaucratic rather than entrepreneurial. Unlike private sector activity, it does not lend itself to clustering effects. Bringing highly paid public service jobs to small towns also makes it tougher for the private sector to recruit good staff. It raises house prices for locals in modestly paid employment. Given the essential nature of interaction between public servants of differing disciplines and perspectives, it also makes it harder for them to do their job.

Announced off-the-hoof in December 2000, decentralisation was unsupported by cost benefit analysis or any preparation. But, aimed at relocating 10,300 public servants away from Dublin, it was expected to greatly boost employment in the regions. But what government needs to do is entice new industries to these regions. Using the inducement of promotion, it is attempting Soviet-style mass relocation. At the time of writing, the policy isn't working. The truth is that it never can. Compared to what a proper policy – a real spatial strategy – would have produced, the economic benefit of spraying 10,300 public service jobs all over the countryside is risible.

Neither are public servants convinced of the benefits to them. By 2006, the public sector trade union IMPACT reported that, of its 1,034 members due to relocate, 876 refuse to move.[9] Of the 383 FÁS staff designated to move, only 66 are willing to go and, in spite of Birr's undoubted charms as a place to live, most of those are motivated by the prospect of promotion. The simple fact is that most semi-state workers are middle-aged and deeply rooted in the communities in which they live, their partners work and their children go to school. Unlike in the private sector, they cannot be fired and have to be incentivised to make the move. But basing promotion on a public servant's willingness to live in Sligo or Athlone means not basing it on their innate ability to do their job. Regional economic benefits aside, decentralisation is going to seriously damage the public service by hampering the ability of government to find experts living in or willing to relocate to those positions.

Consultants Farrell Grant Sparks – hired by IMPACT to estimate the cost of its 876 refuseniks – estimated a cost of €65 million.[10] As far as the whole public service was concerned, it was only the tip of the iceberg. With nine out of every ten of IMPACT's 1,034 members unwilling to move, the number of total refuseniks is likely to be anything between 8,000 and 9,000 – ten times the number of IMPACT members refusing to leave and suggesting a cost of around €650 million. And these are just the direct costs. Key policy making and implementing departments depend on networks of policy knowledge and flows of information that require close physical proximity to operate effectively. Break those up and serious systemic and operational risks could be the end result. The nursing homes scandal[11] – a scandal that cost the taxpayer hundreds of millions of euro – is an example of how a high turnover of staff within the Department of Health – a department at least located in one place – resulted in policy breakdown. What further high cost disasters await the taxpayer from the scattering of ten thousand public service jobs around the country is yet to become clear, but it's unlikely to be a pretty sight.

Demoralisation of civil servants is yet another risk. For many civil servants, expectations for promotion now require them to uproot their families and lives. For those long in harness, the total change in the 'rules of the game' – affecting both location and promotion – comes at a stage in their lives when alternative career options have long since dried up. The potentially huge implications of this disaffection have not been assessed.

In fact the only implications that were assessed were those relating to the revenues and costs of property transactions. Selling the property of public service offices in Dublin and purchasing properties in cheaper regional towns would, in itself, be profitable, or so the government thought. The real issue of basing public service location on ensuring its productivity and efficiency takes a back seat to officially sanctioned land speculation.

In August 2007, the Labour Court ruled that FÁS could not encourage its staff to move to Birr by making promotion conditional on it. The decision has huge ramifications; suddenly the government cannot use the only carrot it has to make the policy work. The already meagre minority willing to decentralise is set to shrink even further. Someone is finally trying to save the government from itself; but it doesn't want to be saved. Such is the power of local interest groups and TDs that the government responded by merely reaffirming its commitment to the policy. A press release issued on 30 August by the Minister for Finance Brian Cowen stated: 'the Government will continue to move ahead with decentralisation and ensure that no public servant is obliged to accept decentralisation against their wishes and that promotion opportunities remain available.' This means that not only will the state have to duplicate the already large number of public servants by hiring extra ones for each one refusing to decentralise, but now it will have to duplicate promotions as well, the cost of which will, as usual, be borne by the taxpayer. Already in a deep hole, the government is digging harder and faster.

BENCHMARKING

The year 2002 saw the publication of the Benchmarking Report.[12] The Report – authored by the Benchmarking Body – was a response to the perception, or suggestion, that public sector workers were being left behind by the boom. It was later to be shown that this was highly doubtful. Even before account is taken of generous pensions and holiday entitlements, there is evidence that public servants remain significantly better off than private sector workers. But with an election in the offing and trade union leaders alert, government politicians knew what was expected of them. As INTO[13] General Secretary and Senator Joe O'Toole put it, benchmarking is 'no more than going to a different ATM. We will punch in the formula and collect the payout.'[14] As usual, the taxpayer is at the other end of the wall. When the report was published it recommended a once-off rise in public sector pay, averaging 8.9 per cent. For certain classes of public servant, the rates of increase were higher; for others, lower. This was on top of existing national pay agreements. The cost to the taxpayer would be €1 billion annually. As the recommended increases were published, it seemed that tribalism was once again winning the day. The most powerful tribes in the partnership system, senior politically powerful staff, got the big increases. The least powerful but arguably more important frontline staff got the least. Within the prison service, for instance, prison officers got increases of 4 per cent, while deputy and assistant governors got 15 per cent. Within nursing, ordinary nurses – the frontliners – got an award of 8 per cent, half the increase given to a director of nursing.

The very nature of the exercise itself was dubious. It was based on the government's unchallenged view that public servants were made worse off relative to the continued bonanza of bonuses and pay increases enjoyed, allegedly, by the private sector. But were they really? The Benchmarking Body analysed the differences in pay, both between the public and private sector, and amongst different types of public sector workers. Controversially, this analysis was not published, causing one member of the body to resign.[15] Four years later, the ESRI made a comprehensive assessment of the differentials in pay prevailing in 2002, before the report's implementation. It found that public servants had, on average, been paid 40 per cent more than private sector workers *before* the Benchmarking Commission reported. Of course, there were wide disparities between different types of public sector workers. Some, but not all, teachers were clearly underpaid, as were some nurses. But, equally, other types of public servant were overpaid. Instead of taking from overpaid and overstaffed parts of the public sector to give to underpaid and understaffed parts, benchmarking involved the public service exacting tribute from the private sector with no measurable improvement in performance. At the time of writing, a second Benchmarking Commission is due to report. Composed largely of former public service employees and reporting just after an election, it has every incentive to pay tribute to the tribe.

As with the Spatial Strategy, decentralisation has become a debacle. TDs celebrate their prowess in smashing up the public service to provide a few measly jobs for their constituencies, jobs that could be provided in many multiples if a proper spatial strategy was implemented. At least if 100 per cent broadband was achieved, some of the worse effects of decentralisation and spatial failure might be mitigated. However, by 2006, only one in five homes in Ireland had broadband access.[16] In Dún Laoghaire-Rathdown – a part of the country where the population is stagnating – access was 40 per cent. In Leitrim – one of the growing areas of the country and one targeted by decentralisation – access was just 7.8 per cent. In 2007 the government has finally committed itself to tackling the broadband problem, but the resources devoted to that goal, €435 million between 2007 and 2013, are dwarfed by the direct cost of decentralisation, a cool €833 million.

So here we are, a nation divided by tribalism. If the tribes are even achieving something that is in their own interest, it might not be so laughable. But, by destroying the ability of central government to rule effectively, the tribes are only undoing themselves. And they are undoing the future.

CHAPTER 6

Cain Slew Abel

Men of the same trade seldom meet together, even for the purposes of amusement, but the conversation turns into a conspiracy against the public.

Adam Smith 1776

WAKE-UP CALL

With competitive markets, a rising tide lifts all boats. Without them, prosperity lifts prices more than it lifts real incomes. Ireland's prolonged boom occurred before what economists refer to as the microeconomy had been reformed. From the cost of insurance to the price of food and drink, Ireland was one of Europe's more expensive countries even before the full power of the boom. Successive government reports urged greater competition across a range of markets. In air travel and telecommunications there was some success. But, as the economy began to take off in the early 1990s, too many markets were unreformed. The tribes didn't want it. Benchmarking proves that the most powerful tribe is the public sector. Backed by social partnership, the public sector has power far beyond the value it contributes to the economy. But it is far from being the only powerful tribe.

By 2003, Ireland's cost of living was 15 per cent higher than the EU average.[1] Most of this happened in the short period that followed the boom. Using the Harmonised Index of Consumer Prices

(HICP), Ireland's price level had, between 1999 and 2003, risen 9 per cent faster than the EU average. But the HICP excluded the rising cost of mortgage interest relief, a real cost facing borrowers in a country where three-quarters of the population are home owners. According to the Consumer Price Index (CPI), the extent of the rise would have been even higher.

A second bout of high inflation hit the economy in 2005 and, by 2007, Ireland's competitiveness had further declined. Like a weather vane, the multinational sector is sending out ominous signals as of 2007. This sector accounts for over 90,000 jobs in the economy's traded sector – the sector most exposed to international competition. When competitiveness declines, the traded sector is hit the most. It is also the economy's most productive sector. Although it accounts for only one-third of manufacturing employment, it produces two-thirds of that sector's output. Early in 2007, Pfizer, Xerox and several other multinationals announced their intentions to scale back their operations here. Rising costs in Ireland, coupled with the rising number of alternative low cost locations, were the key reason.

In 1995, Ireland was ranked the eighth most expensive country in the Eurozone.[2] About to lose control of its currency by adopting the euro, Ireland needed to keep inflation as low as possible to stay competitive. It was failing. From being ranked fourth in the Eurozone, Ireland's ranking in the cost of living league had risen to 'a possible second' place in 2002, according to state agency Forfás. Official politeness cannot mask the facts: Ireland is rapidly becoming the most expensive country in the Eurozone. Food prices in Ireland are on average 25 per cent higher than the EU average – an embarrassment for a country with a supposed advantage in food production. From seventh place in 2000, today Ireland's position in the world competitiveness rankings has fallen seven places to fourteenth place.[3]

The government's response to the rising cost of living is to blame rising oil prices and interest rates. But these are realities faced by most of Ireland's competitors. It is the microeconomy – everything from the level of taxes needed to fund central government, local authority government and the public sector – that explains Ireland's falling international competitiveness.

CAIN SLEW ABEL

In the Old Testament story Cain kills his brother Abel. The story is a good analogy for what is happening to the Irish economy today. Like any economy, Ireland's economy is divided into two sectors: the traded sector and the non-traded sector. The word 'traded' refers to the fact that firms operating in this sector trade their goods and services internationally. They face many challenges that the domesticated non-traded sector does not, including tough international competition, exchange rate turbulence and a more rapid pace of technological change. The traded sector relies heavily on the non-traded sector for its competitiveness. In this sense, the non-traded sector can describe any part of the domestic economy that is protected from international competition but which influences companies that are not. In Ireland today, property prices, electricity charges and local authority charges are just some examples of how the non-traded sector affects our international competitiveness. And if there are commercial pressures in the non-traded sector, they are often dampened by government intervention that acts to strangle competition.

A breakdown of inflation trends, published in July 2007,[4] shows just how Cain is slaying Abel. In the twelve months to that month inclusive, general prices, as measured by the CPI, rose by 5 per cent.[5] In the cut-throat internationally traded clothing and footwear sector, prices actually *fell* by 1.4 per cent. Furniture products and household goods had also fallen in price, by over 1 per cent, while increased competition in the telecommunications market was also bringing prices down. Contrary to some strong opponents of competition, this is not coming at the cost of job losses. In fact, retail employment is growing strongly in 2007[6] and, at 4.5 per cent, unemployment is close to historic lows.

Had it been left up to the traded sector, Irish inflation would be close to zero, possibly even negative, helping to improve the economy's ability to raise employment and productivity even further. Because of the non-traded sector, this isn't happening. Relative inflation data proves it. While other Eurozone countries take the interest rate rises in their stride,[7] Ireland's chronically high house prices – a function of the problems discussed in the previous chapter – acts like a magnifying glass on a ray of sun, burning the Irish consumer. Oil price increases are also felt by Ireland's competitors. But Ireland's overreliance on the car rather than public transport makes their impact particularly sharp.[8] As a result, the category of the CPI capturing this effect[9] showed rises in mid-2007 by over twenty per cent a year. Prices in the alcoholic beverages and tobacco sector are rising by over 5 per cent, mainly due to a 50 cent rise in the duty on tobacco introduced in December 2006.

This is just the tip of the iceberg. The government also controls the level of local authority charges, public transport fares, hospital charges and health insurance charges, among other things, and the huge impact this is having on Ireland's competitiveness can only be grasped by looking at inflation over a longer period of time.

Between January 2000 and July 2007 the CPI – a guide to the cost of living – rose by 34.6 per cent. In the competitive traded sector, price growth was flat or negative. Clothing and footwear prices fell by 21.1 per cent. Food prices rose, but by less than inflation, up 18.3 per cent. The contrast with the other side of the economy was astonishing. When combined in a single category, prices of water supply, refuse collection and local authority service charges – all areas controlled by the state – rose by an incredible 255.4 per cent. Hospital service charges rose by 101.4 per cent and education costs by 60.7 per cent. As exporters were struggling with falling prices internationally, the state was aggressively pushing up their costs.

These increases are hardly funding any increase in public sector productivity. The output of the public sector is rising, but this is because of a huge increase in public sector employment, rather than any rise in productivity. Having pledged to cut public sector numbers by 5,000, the 2002–2007 Fianna Fáil-Progressive Democrat government actually increased them by 55,000. In some areas – teaching, for example – increases in staff numbers were justified by a rising population. As late as 2006, an OECD report pointed to high primary school class sizes as something holding the economy back[10] (the same report was, however, politely damning about the value for money being received from the public sector).

The OECD report noted that, while Ireland was close to the top of the league for economic well-being, this was because it 'relied to a large extent on foreign corporations as the main generator of research'. Education policy is just one area where the state's inability to reform is testing the resolve of multinational companies here, companies who are looking for well-trained staff for the high quality and highly paid jobs they are bringing here. The OECD didn't mince words when it reported that education outcomes in Ireland, while acceptable, remain 'far below the results achieved by the best performers in the OECD'. It added that 'Further efforts at all levels ... are needed to bring the education system to best practice.'

The report called for the re-introduction of third level fees and institutional reforms to make universities streamlined and meritocratic. But, as the report made its recommendations, powerful and influential vested interests were resisting far more modest developments. By 2006, a practice called 'poaching' was becoming more frequent in Irish universities. Frustrated by bureaucracy and inertia, academics with good records in badly run universities were being 'poached' by universities that were more meritocratic. In any well-functioning economy, this practice is essential to ensure that the talents of good people are not wasted by badly-run organisations. It also serves as an important means of keeping management in check. Well-run organisations hold managers to account if they lose good staff. Despite its pejorative name, a persistent occurrence of 'poaching' of staff is a crucial signal that managers are not handling their staff well. But universities are having none of it and, under the auspices of social partnership, the presidents of Ireland's seven universities met together in 2006 to endorse an agreement restricting the practice.

But if education is a place where the Ireland of the 1950s has managed to survive, it is a bastion of modernity compared to some other sectors. Another powerful tribe – the Licensed Vintners Association – had, for decades, fiercely and successfully resisted proposals to overhaul licensing laws that dated from the nineteenth century. Economist Cathal Guiomard noted in 1995 that there were then as many pubs in Ireland as there had been at the turn of the century, despite a much higher population. In fact, Guiomard was understating things: there are barely more pubs in modern Ireland than there had been in the 1690s – a time when the population of the country was around one million.

By 2006, the country's population had risen further still and a proposal was made by the Minister for Justice Michael McDowell to expand consumer choice by introducing Café Bar licenses. He was to meet stiff resistance. Any limit to the supply of a profitable license causes that license to have a value. It is one of the reasons why licenses to trade should never have a numerical restriction.[11] Some years previously, the government accepted this principle by deregulating the taxi industry. By the late 1990s, the failure of public transport, combined with the pressures of population growth and rising affluence stretched queues for taxis beyond the limits of endurance. Reform was inevitable. If the case for deregulating the drinks industry was strong, the cost of doing so to the pub trade would be high. By the late 1990s, pub licenses – pieces of paper originally nearly worthless – were changing hands for millions of euros.

The growing number of young people with money to spend is feeding a huge growth in profits. With alcohol prices rising much faster than inflation, deregulation is also needed to lower prices. Compared to a rise of 30 per cent in the general price level between the start of 1997 and end of 2006, the price of alcohol had risen by 45 per cent. The reason is clear: there is a lack of competition. While the population rose by almost one-third between 1971 and 1998, the number of pub licenses remained static. The result was that the gross margins of public houses rose from 20 per cent in 1971 – already high by international standards – to over 40 per cent in 1998.[12]

There are added reasons for reforming. Finding themselves living in newly created commuter-belt towns, many young people are now denied the chance to walk to a local pub. Quite apart from the price issue, the need to improve the quality of life of hundreds of thousands of people is the strongest reason of all for reform, a fact underlined by the growing incidence of road deaths. In short, the arguments for reform are too powerful to ignore.

Unfortunately, there are even more powerful forces at work. To a man and woman, TDs in government and in opposition Fine Gael[13] have backed the drinks' lobby, arguing that reform would lead to more alcoholism amongst young people. If it wasn't so hypocritical, the argument would be laughable. The high cost of drinking in pubs has caused sales of alcohol from retail outlets to soar. The fact is that, for many in commuter-belt Ireland, there is no pub within walking distance, making drinking at home the only option. Far from encouraging alcoholism, creating new pub licenses would allow drinking to occur in a healthier setting, one where the social dimension – conversation and atmosphere – puts alcohol in a more wholesome context.

But what most exposed the hollow nature of the argument was the government's decision, made within months of opposition to reform, to drop proposals in the Alcohol Products Bill aimed at restricting alcohol advertising. Concern about under-age drinking – and pressure for action – had been growing since a 2002 *Prime Time* exposé of teenage drinking in Ireland. The government proposed, among other things, to ban alcohol advertising on television until after 9.00 p.m. Following over three years of extensive lobbying,[14] the government caved in to producer interests.

CONSUMERS FIGHT BACK

By the autumn of 2005, public cynicism about the government's fondness for vested interest groups reached a fever pitch. In an opinion poll in September of that year, 93 per cent of respondents said they believed they were being 'ripped off'.[15]

Over the late summer and early autumn Eddie Hobbs – former finance spokesman for the Consumer Association of Ireland (CAI) and sudden consumer televangelist – had been rousing television audiences around the country with a regular programme entitled *Rip-Off Republic*. A blistering exposé of Ireland's rising cost of living, one issue it focused on became a lightning conductor for public anger: the Groceries Order. Preventing wholesalers from passing the value of bulk discounts on processed food to retailers, the Order was a way of keeping a floor under prices. Several government reports recommended its abolition. But politicians stood in fear of the food industry. In 1994, the Irish Business and Employers Confederation (IBEC) claimed that abolishing it would lead to 'commercial terrorism'.[16] Over a decade later, hysterical arguments against the abolition were still being used.[17] As the Hobbs phenomenon showed, the rest of the country had moved on. But resistance amongst backbench TDs to reform was still strong in the Dáil, a place where producers generally have a louder voice than consumers.

But if producer interests had the edge when it came to lobbying, people power was slowly asserting itself. In September 2005, an opinion poll showed the government's popularity slumping to 32 per cent, a drop of almost 10 percentage points since the 2002 general election. The Celtic Tiger had awoken a sleeping tiger. Fuel and electricity prices, health charges and pub prices were increasingly seen as examples of a helpless public being exploited by a cabal of monopolists, with politicians holding their hats and coats as they did so. Someone was getting the lion's share of the tiger's growth and – as far as consumers were concerned – it wasn't them.

Minister for Enterprise Trade and Employment Micheál Martin was already in the process of taking action. That November, his Department produced incontrovertible evidence that countries without such an Order had lower processed food price inflation than those that did. By December, it was clear that the government was going to abolish the Order.

By March of 2007 – a year after the abolition took effect – it was clear that the move was working. Against a tide of rising inflation, the price of processed foods once covered by the Order is registering the largest year-on-year fall in four years.[18] The message to be taken from this is clear: reform works. The Groceries Order is a small example of what needs to be done on a much broader scale. Huge swathes of the Irish economy are subject to restrictive practices and outdated protection. If the slow speed of reform to date reflects a historical tolerance of high prices on the part of consumers, it doesn't look like lasting. With the public hard bitten by the cost of living, the poor mouth arguments used in favour of protectionism are gradually wearing thin. More educated and informed of their own interests, consumers are willing to hold politicians to account. Just as politicians who dared to reform were at risk twenty years ago, the time will come when those who don't are at risk.

Confronting the small town mentality of local and national monopolists will always be a huge problem but there is an even bigger and related problem: the small size of the towns themselves.

PART III

FUTURE POSITIVE

As you go through life, there are thousands of little forks in the road, and there are a few really big forks – those moments of reckoning, moments of truth.

Lee Iacocca

CHAPTER 7

The Only Way is Up

All things good of this earth flow into the city.

Pericles of Athens, around 450 BC

WE JUST DON'T GET IT

It is 5,000 years since the world's first city was created in modern day Iraq. It is 2,500 years since the Greek politician Pericles raved about cities. But, instead of properly urbanising, modern Ireland's main conurbations are evolving into collections of large villages. Slowly, the consequences are becoming clear. Regions lack critical mass. Populations are thinly spread. Public services are not cost efficient. Markets are too dominated by local monopolists. In other words, most of the problems still endemic in our economy and society can be traced to a single factor: a failure to properly urbanise.

But, in an age of rising environmental awareness, perhaps the most awesome result is this: despite one of the lowest rates of car ownership in the EU, Ireland consumes 50 per cent more oil per head for transportation than the EU average. If further conclusive proof is needed of the failure of spatial planning in Ireland, this is it. Ireland's low and badly distributed population density is turning its economy into an oil junkie.

As census data from the CSO confirms, Ireland is a nation suffering a second famine – a time famine. Commutes to work are getting longer and house buyers are desperately searching for accommodation near public transport. As leading economist George Lee has pointed out, of around €4 billion worth of oil imported annually, some 70 per cent is now used for cars. This share compares with 41 per cent in 1994. Between 1990 and 2005, Ireland's transport energy needs grew almost five times faster than the European average, and more than six times faster than Denmark's – a state comparable to Ireland in terms of size – and over seven times faster than the UK's.[1]

The irony is that our dislike of urban centres stems from a belief that rural living is a good thing and that urbanisation threatens it. The first belief is correct, rural living is a good thing. Against its economic advantages, city life carries with it stresses and strains that damage a country's cultural and moral fabric. Where our policy makers have got it wrong is in their assumptions that urban and rural living are mutually exclusive and hostile alternatives. Far from threatening rural life, urbanisation enhances it by ensuring that cities grow within their limits, through building up, rather than out, thus protecting rural areas from urban sprawl.

ICH BIN EIN BERLINER

As Ireland grappled with the advance of free market capitalism, a debate raged over whether Ireland's economy should emulate social democratic Germany or the robust capitalism of the US. The debate – styled 'Boston or Berlin' – had the right title but the wrong subject matter. Ireland's economic model is a happy compromise between Germany's chronically excessive taxation and smothering welfare and the harsh indifference of the US economy; a model that allows for a dynamic, full-employment economy, but with a social welfare system in the European mould.

We do need a debate on which country to emulate, but not as regards the economy. The 'Boston or Berlin' debate we do need concerns the shape of our cities and how we want them to look. It's not an either/or choice. The Dublin skyline will need to contain elements of both Boston and Berlin. The idea of skyscraper apartments spanning the entire city skyline is too far-fetched; we are barely getting used to the idea that apartments were not just for students. Fortunately, achieving the density dividend doesn't require Boston skylines. But if Irish citizens are to be able buy affordable property within reasonable distance of family, friends and work then we have to accept that we can have low house prices or skylines, but not both.

A few kilometres north of Berlin's city centre, the district of Prenzlauer Berg is experiencing something rare in German cities these days: a baby boom. Spacious and well designed, with good facilities and plenty of green space, it is a district dominated by apartment blocks, homes that few Irish people would ever consider raising families in. On the ground floors of these buildings – often seven or eight storeys high – can be found baker shops, hairdressers, newsagents, pharmacies and cafés. Beside them are playgrounds where young children can enjoy space and contact with nature. Close by, within walking distance or a few minutes by (excellent) public transport, are cinemas, bars and restaurants that allow their parents to stay young. The Berliner can waltz around his or her city with little effort. Like most European capitals, Berlin is a city built according to the density dividend. Within a kilometre radius of his or her dwelling, most residents of this city can find most of the things they need to sustain a meaningful and high quality existence. On top of this – and this is really incomprehensible to us – German tenancy laws permit Berliners to live their lives and raise families without the need to own property.

The population density of Berlin is around 3,800 per square kilometre. Covering a land mass of 890 square kilometres, it accommodates 3.8 million people with not a skyscraper in sight. County Dublin – now de facto Dublin City – covers almost the same land mass and holds 1.2 million people in a space of land, 922 square kilometres, that is little bigger than Berlin's. Ironically, in the late eighteenth century, Dublin was more populous than Berlin.

Now a hectare of land in Berlin supports, on average, three times the population of a Dublin hectare. The implications go far beyond the cost of purchasing property. A kilometre of public transport – be it road or rail – in Berlin serves, on average, three times the number of commuters than it does in Dublin. A café or pub or pharmacy in Berlin is likely to have significantly more people within a walkable radius than a Dublin one. The costs of doing business are likely to be spread over a greater number of customers. Prices – other things being equal – are likely to be lower. The effect on economic productivity is also positive. A builder in Berlin extracts, on average, considerably more value per hectare than one in Dublin. The productivity benefit has another dimension: more efficiently clustered, Berliners are in a better position to form and maintain the kind of business and civic associations that are the basis of any flourishing city economy.

In contrast with Berlin, less than half of Dublin's inhabitants live in the area formally known as Dublin City.[2] This assumes that Dublin is defined by Dublin County. Beyond that county border are anything between a half and three-quarters of a million persons whose livelihoods depend on economic activity in the capital. But, instead of drawing them in towards its centre, Dublin is pushing them away. Compared to 2.1 per cent within the city limits, Lucan's population has risen by 24 per cent in four years, Sandyford's population by 20 per cent, Kilmacud's by 23 per cent, Swords' by 25 per cent and Rush's by 22 per cent. By contrast, the population of many areas close to the city centre – Crumlin, for instance – is falling when it should be rising. By 2006, the ESRI reported that, of some 135,439 working between Dublin's Royal and Grand canals – the central core of the city – only 15,619 were living there.[3]

Officially in Meath but now de facto a part of Dublin's economic zone, Stamullen's recent growth is a typical example of the flipside of this. In 2007, a newspaper article on the town's development reported that, in the town, 'winding country roads without footpaths lead past newly-built suburban estates to a main street where many of the people appear to be working on nearby building sites.'[4] From just 779 souls in 2002, Stamullen's population rose to 2487 by

2006.[5] By the following year, three out of four of the houses in the town had been built in the previous five years. The Saturday bus service had been stopped years before – just as it was on the verge of becoming more necessary. There is no slip road to the nearby M1 motorway. Train services are, as is usual in most of Ireland, inadequate. The article quoted a resident of the town saying, 'you have to have a car to live here.'

Living in most small towns in Germany or Holland without a car is not ideal. But – as the author knows from personal experience – it is possible to do so without major inconvenience. Ireland's sprawled development is forcing further congestion on roads, and creating an ever larger carbon footprint. The collateral damage from this has spread beyond transport. It now impacts on the cost of living and the quality of life in the country. Despite a fourfold increase in population, in 2007 Stamullen still has only one pub. The grip of the licensing laws would ensure that – as far as drinking out is concerned – its citizens are deprived of a competitive market. Thanks to poor transport planning – and despite being just a mile away – the nearest alternative pub is unreachable by foot during the evenings because of a lack of footpaths. Too far from the city to enjoy what it has to offer, but no longer small enough to be charmingly rural, towns like Stamullen are falling between two stools. Rather than protecting it, our present approach to urbanisation is destroying country life.

Cup Cakes and Doughnuts

What is happening in Stamullen is not happening in Dublin. One-third less densely populated than Berlin,[6] Dublin has huge potential to densify itself by drawing population into its centre. Dublin's hardest working area – one of the hardest working areas in the country, in fact – is Swords. Three-quarters of Swords' population is in the labour market. In Navan, Balbriggan and Naas – other commuter towns – the figure is around 72 per cent. The populations of these towns need to be located in the city centre. By contrast, Dublin's centre contains many areas with low labour force participation. Having reaped a huge gain during the property boom, many of its residents don't need to work anymore. Many others are retired.

As a result, while commuter towns are surging, Dublin City's population rose by just 2.1 per cent between 2002 and 2006.[7] With the cost of even a two-bedroom terraced house in Dublin rising over €500,000, an ever widening range of young workers – teachers and nurses especially – are fleeing the capital. Schools are losing good teaching staff. A teacher's starting salary is around €32,000, less than one-tenth of the average house price in Dublin.

Dublin is now a doughnut city: a city where the most rapid growth – and most of the apartment building – is occurring around the fringes. It ought to be a cup-cake city, with a skyline rising in the centre and falling away at the edges. Although nowhere is as chronic as Dublin, the problem is still widespread across the country. As its hinterland expanded rapidly, Cork City's population actually fell by 3 per cent between 2002 and 2006, as did Limerick's. Waterford's population grew by a disappointing 2.5 per cent. Only Galway City's population grew by something approximating to the national trend.[8]

The west will suffer from this more than most regions. As an extensive analyses[9] of the economic challenges faced by that region of Ireland noted in 1999, western counties[10] 'make up 37 per cent of the country's land mass, they account for only 9.6 per cent of Ireland's net output' and that their 'small existing industrial base is prone to decline'. The report also noted that the population density of the region was twenty-five persons per square kilometre. Bigger in land size than the state of Israel – home to seven million people – this area once held a more modest two million people. But with four-fifths of its population of around 700,000 living outside urban areas, it had now only one town with more than 50,000. The report noted the region's infrastructure deficit and need for more investment. It also noted its high dependence on traditional sectors. The most telling observation of all was the following: 'Within the west there is a substantial variation … with value added in manufacturing, building and construction accounting for over 40 per cent of total output in Galway as against 10 per cent in Leitrim and Clare.' Unfortunately – perhaps because it had no mandate to – the report never joined the dots. Yes, the west drastically needed more economic diversity. But the diversity that did exist existed in the one area with some urbanisation. What the west needed – and still needs – is not more sprawl. What the west needed – and still needs – is a bigger, more densely packed city.

THE ONLY WAY IS UP

The 'Manhattanisation' of Dublin is on no-one's agenda. But it has to be admitted that – to the outside observer at least – most Irish towns look more like loosely connected villages than urban centres. In March 2005, Dublin businessman Denis O'Brien appealed a decision by the City Council to stop him building a 25-storey residential development to state planning agency An Bord Pleanála. Nestled between Herbert Park and Morehampton Road in Dublin's Donnybrook are a series of charming one- and two-storey redbrick houses. About the same distance from the city centre as Prenzlauer Berg is from Berlin's, these houses epitomise the tension between the modern vision of Ireland's towns and the old one. It is quite possible to sympathise with the latter. How could anyone not want to live in a row of redbrick houses where everyone knows each other, where the village pub and shop is around the corner and from where you can walk to town in half an hour?

The trouble is that everybody does but nobody can. In Prenzlauer Berg, young couples live in well-designed buildings. Strong rights of tenure mean that many young German couples don't even have to worry about buying the place in which they live; good apartments can be rented for under €1,000 a month. Germany is one country where the density dividend is working.[11] In Ireland, the Bull McCabe mentality has spread from rural areas and into the most unrural parts of cities (see Chapter 10). At the height of the property boom of 2005, two-bedroom single-storey redbrick houses in Donnybrook – barely adequate for two people let alone a family – were selling for

€600,000. In Prenzlauer Berg, decent apartments of larger size, if not quite as charming, were selling for €150,000. The fact that Donnybrook was four times more expensive didn't reflect the snob factor. Both Donnybrook and Prenzlauer Berg are considered desirable parts of their respective cities. It simply reflected the fact that the average skyline in Berlin was several storeys higher. Builders in Berlin are – without ruining the skyline – permitted to make far more efficient use of development land than builders in Dublin. So far, business competitiveness in cities like Berlin is held back by high taxation. Ireland's trouble is that this advantage, relative to other countries, can vanish at the stroke of a foreign finance minister's pen. Its disadvantage – the high cost of land and property – will take longer to overcome.

As of 2005, O'Brien and property tycoon Sean Dunne were – for commercial rather than altruistic motives – doing what was necessary to get the ball rolling. O'Brien's proposal was turned down on grounds of 'excessive height and scale'. In November of that year, Dunne purchased the site of the Berkeley Court Hotel – an upmarket hotel in Dublin's sought after Ballsbridge – for €119 million, or approximately €58 million per acre. This was four times the average price of land in London, one of the most expensive capital cities internationally.[12]

How had it come to this? In 1974 the so-called Kenny Report urged the government to cap the price of land. Too politically sensitive, the report was never implemented, although Taoiseach Bertie Ahern hinted at doing so in 2002. There are good grounds for capping land where family housing is being developed, as was done in the UK, where land zoned for such development by local authorities became de facto a monopoly good. Although some regard capping land prices as state intervention, in the UK even free market economists accepted that monopoly power was something to be curtailed by state intervention. Making land available for housing is socially vital to give families a decent quality of life.

In town centres the challenges and opportunities are different. Even the highest price for land is sustainable once developers are allowed to realize the maximum value from the site concerned by building up and spreading the land cost over more square metres of property in the process. Building up makes social and economic sense as well. As mentioned in Chapter 3, creating dense clusters of efficient communities where people and businesses can enjoy low cost access to each other, is crucial to achieving the density dividend.

Like O'Brien before him, Dunne developed a proposal to build a 37-storey apartment building on his new site. Commentators observed that the proposal, if allowed to go ahead, would 'change forever the aesthetics of the area'. For hundreds of thousands of rugby fans around the world, Ballsbridge is famous as the good-natured and easygoing home to Lansdowne Road, the venue for most of Ireland's matches. Situated on the picturesque River Dodder, it is home to some of Dublin's finest restaurants and best-loved pubs. But as a suburb lying on key commuter routes, it is also the kind of area that, in any other city, would be brimming with young people. From a city planning point of view, building up makes absolute sense. For those living there, the idea is under-standably anathema. The debate on the issue is as uncoordinated as the skyline it concerns. For a place like Donnybrook – some-where between having both single-storey redbrick houses and forty storey buildings – there must be a compromise that retains the area's character while densifying its population. For more central parts of the city, the arguments for high rise buildings are much stronger.

Slowly but surely, the penny appears to be dropping. In September 2007, Dublin City Council approved planning guide-lines that would require builders to increase the size of new apart-ments by 25 per cent.[13] In an effort to accommodate families, the guidelines require half of all apartment complexes to be at least eighty square metres in size and include rules on the size of kitchens, bedrooms and public space. What a pity that, at the time this measure was finally passed, there were 216,000 vacant dwellings in the state (see Chapter 3).

PLANNING FOR THE DENSITY DIVIDEND

The failure to target the growth of major cities to rival Dublin is a major blow to the density dividend. But, fortunately, it is also reversible. Huge population flows would not only fill existing vacant dwellings over the next decades; provided the economy's productivity improves, it would also justify additional building, and building up in our urban centres – the kind of building we should have been doing more of in the last few decades. The National Spatial Strategy is a major reason why we haven't done this. Divisive and dysfunctional, the approach of hub and non-hub towns has failed to densify the urban centres properly.

It is a goal that can be achieved without undermining the future of smaller towns. A strategic application of the National Development Plan can put the populations of these smaller towns within reasonable commuting distances of the jobs and activities their populations want access to. In a country where no place is more than eighty kilometres from the coast, achieving this shouldn't be rocket science.

From spreading the population like confetti, the goal of the Spatial Strategy needs to shift towards the creation of significant major cities. Even without the historic population growth rates predicted in Chapter 1, the scope will be there to do it. According to projections by the CSO, the state's population will rise to just over five million by 2020. Between 2002 and 2006, the joint populations of Cork and Limerick (cities and suburban areas) and Galway and Waterford cities rose by just 4 per cent,[14] half the national growth rate of 8 per cent recorded in that period.

If that relationship were reversed in the coming decades, something remarkable would happen. By 2020, Cork City and its immediate suburbs would be home to just over 300,000 people, Limerick and its immediate suburbs to 136,000, Galway to 114,000 and Waterford to 72,000. Assuming that its population rose at the same rate as the national average, the Shannon region's population would rise to 428,000 by 2020. Instead of setting specific city targets like these, the Spatial Strategy targets growth in cities and their 'hinter-lands'. The needed focus on densification is absent. Various esti-mates for population growth after 2020 predict a rise to six million by 2050. Chapter 1 gave reasons why this could well be a conser-vative number, but it is a useful benchmark. A real spatial strategy – one aggressively targeting urban growth – could achieve an improved distribution of population as early as 2020.

Continuing that redistribution would eventually lead to the pop-ulation of these cities, of their own volition, growing faster than the national rate. Were these urban areas to grow just 1.2 times faster than the nation as a whole, Cork City and suburbs would contain over half a million people, Limerick almost one quarter of a million, Galway almost 200,000 and Waterford City over 125,000. Repeating the assumption that the Shannon region grows at the same rate as the national population, its population would reach 538,000, while that of Connacht would reach 750,000.

As has been shown, a rise in the state's population to nine million by the middle of the decade is conceivable. The scenarios painted above for the possible future sizes of Irish cities are modest, if not small, by the standards of cities in many other small countries. But they do go a long way towards the realization of the density dividend in cities other than Dublin. Were they to be achieved, Ireland – both as a country with reasonable but still modest population densities, but also as one of the world's properly citied nations – would have, at long last, arrived.

CHAPTER 8

Shannon versus Shenzhen

Reliance on government rather than self-reliance has become so ingrained in the public psyche that it tends to be assumed that nobody can act unless government can act.

Professor Joe Lee

The question is not whether to be angry. The question is why to be angry, when to be angry and with whom to be angry.

Ancient Greek wisdom

THE WEST'S AWAKE

Few episodes highlight the need to densify Ireland's population more than the 2007 debate on the future of the Shannon region. Home to some two million people in the 1840s, the area west of the Shannon has failed to share fully in Ireland's economy. The facts speak for themselves. The highest rate of unemployment in the country, over 15.8 per cent, occurs in the western town of Ballina. The counties of the west and north-west – among the most sparsely populated – have the highest rates of poverty and alienation.[1] In parts of it, the west remains a place where the 1980s survives. To some, this is Dublin's fault, a legacy of willful neglect by east-coast elites. To some of the elites, it reflects a failure to switch regional economic attitudes from self-pity to self-reliance. The truth is in-between. The

west has been mismanaged, not neglected. That mismanagement reflects as much an excess of intervention as a lack of it.

To make it more attractive to international business, Aer Lingus has held slots at London's Heathrow Airport, a situation under-pinned by a government that, until 2007, owned the airline. Having ended the stopover rule a year earlier as part of the Open Skies Agreement,[2] the government privatised Aer Lingus in 2007, but held a 25 per cent stake in the company. The Rule required a mini-mum share of flights between the US and Ireland that had to stop at or begin at Shannon. Soon after privatisation, the airline's manage-ment announced that the Heathrow slot was being relocated to Belfast Airport. Within a year, eight decades of protectionism in the airline industry came to an end. The storm of criticism was pre-dictable: Minister for Defence Willie O'Dea – a representative for nearby Limerick City – likened the decision to the genocide of Oliver Cromwell and predicted economic 'Armageddon' for the area. That September, a vote was taken in the Dáil calling on the government to demand an extraordinary general meeting of Aer Lingus. A group called the Atlantic Connectivity Alliance warned local TDs that if they failed to vote for the measure they would 'suf-fer politically'. Several government TDs absented themselves from the Dáil as a result.

The government did endorse a report concluding that the loss of the direct Shannon-Heathrow connection would have 'a negative impact on connectivity to/from the region'. It supported the idea of creating a 'second major metropolitan corridor on the island of Ireland to complement and counterbalance the strengthening Dublin-Belfast corridor'. But no-one asked why the Dublin-Belfast corridor was so strong in the first place. The approach was based on forcing economic activity where it refused to go of its own volition – the same logic that stunted Ireland's growth in the past – instead of tackling the root causes of its reluctance.

Born in County Tipperary, Tony Ryan[3] was a native of the Shannon and Mid-Western region. Like many talented people of his generation, Ryan joined Aer Lingus as a young man. Combining as it did a mix of job security with a commercial work environment, Aer Lingus was one of the few companies worth working for in an otherwise stagnant age.[4] By the early 1970s, Ryan had acquired a reputation as one of Aer Lingus' toughest and most capable salesmen.

In the 1960s, Greek shipping magnates made millions by exploiting their country's dependence on the sea. They hadn't allowed Greece's relative isolation – but for underdeveloped Turkey it was landlocked by communism – nor its absence from the EEC to stop them. Despite being one of Europe's only two island nations, Ireland's record in navigation and shipping has always been poor. But it had another kind of dependence that was ripe for exploitation and Ryan spotted it.

Leveraging international contacts gained leasing aircraft for Aer Lingus, Ryan set up Guiness Peat Aviation (GPA) in 1975. Worried by the region's economic underdevelopment, the government encouraged Ryan to set up the company in Shannon, later claiming that it would become like Shenzhen province in China, the first region of that country to be designated a 'Special Economic Zone' by China's communist leadership. The comparison was ironic. Highly populated, Shenzhen province was home to over eighteen million people. From a population of under a third of a million in 1980 – far larger than that of Limerick City but comparable to the population of the mid-west – Shenzhen City's population had grown to just under 8.5 million by 2006.[5] Spread over a comparable, if not smaller, land size than that of Limerick, some thirty square kilometres, Shenzhen is at an arguably unacceptable extreme of the population density spectrum.[6] But with barely more than 50,000 people in its defined limits, Limerick City is at the other.

A motorway built in Shenzhen would be used by a hundred times more people than one built in Shannon. Broadband is another case in point. The spray-gun development of Ireland's population has made investment in the infrastructure required to provide it uneconomic. By contrast, Asia's densely populated cities justify investment in wireless zones, the catchment areas of which can exceed several million, making the per unit cost of provision negligible.

The government's dream for the aircraft leasing industry was to partly come true. A thriving aircraft leasing industry did develop in Ireland. But the fact that it was concentrated around Dublin rather than around the desired Shannon region cast light on the real problem facing the west: the unattractiveness of doing business in such a low population region. For aircraft leasing, that unattractiveness was related to the fact that, by comparison, Dublin was well served by other providers of high value added services on which it depended to do business.

Aer Lingus' decision to relocate its Heathrow slots was a sheer numbers game.[7] Belfast boasts over 300,000 people in its urban area and 700,000 in its immediate catchment area.[8] When put together with their immediate suburbs, Limerick City and the town of Shannon could scrape 100,000 people between them. If their wider economic hinterlands[9] were added, that figure would rise to 361,000.[10] But this population is spread over a sizable land mass poorly connected by transport. There are over a million people who could get to Belfast with the same ease. For an industry with such high fixed costs, these figures make a massive difference to a company's ability to drown those costs in sheer passenger volumes.

For Aer Lingus shareholders, there was little doubt where a slot at Heathrow should be used. Instead of blaming Aer Lingus, local interests might have asked a different question: in a state whose population grew by 8 per cent in the four short years between 2002 and 2006 – when the full panoply of supports for Shannon Airport were still in operation – why was the National Spatial Strategy targeting growth in five towns in the nearby region[11] instead of achieving real critical mass in Limerick? Between 1996 and 2006, the population of the hinterland area of Limerick City grew by almost 44,000. Had half of this growth been channeled into Limerick City, it would be on its way to becoming worthy of the title 'city'.

THE RYANAIR GENERATION

There is a cultural dimension to Ireland's air industry story. In March 2007, a business venture of Tony Ryan's founded in 1985, Ryanair, was declared by the International Air Transport Association to be the world's largest international airline. Initially, state support was part of this success. But, fundamentally, it is a story that shows just what Ireland can do when the energy and ability of its best people are released. Two of Tony Ryan's business progenies, Denis O'Brien of Communicorp and Ryanair Chief Excecutive Michael O'Leary have continued the story. Together they are helping to redefine and reshape a business and economic future that their detractors held back for so long.

Having been pilloried by some in the media for being heartless, O'Leary has been been a saint compared to his rivals. After all, what could have been more heartless than the action of Aer Lingus when, between 1980 and 1985, it relentlessly pushed up its fares, a move adding significantly to the misery of emigrants who relied upon the airline to visit family and friends back home. This contrasts sharply with what Ryanair is doing: reducing the cost of foreign travel to the price of an evening meal.

O'Brien is also showing how entrepreneurs, rather than state monopolies, are benefiting ordinary people. His entry into the telecommunications market laid foundations for a durable decline in the cost of telecommunications in Ireland. By setting up Newstalk 106–108 fm, he has replaced a monopolistic national broadcast market with a dynamic and competitive one.

Ireland must choose between failure and success. Chinese population densities are not desirable in terms of the quality of life they present. But neither is it feasible to expect an economic zone to flourish with as few people as the Shannon region. Where spatial planning and urban density is concerned, Ireland will have to find a compromise between Shannon and Shenzhen.

Compromises must be found in other areas. Instead of demonising successful business people, Ireland's model of social partnership must take the likes of O'Brien and O'Leary on board. If not, the ground will be laid for a battle for Ireland's future, between dynamism and expansion on the one side and backward-looking statism on the other. Thankfully, as the relocation of the Heathrow slot from Shannon to Belfast has shown, the government is finally recognising the reality of a modern competitive economy. The motion for it to call an extraordinary general meeting of Aer Lingus was defeated. Slowly and politely, but strategically and firmly, the poor mouth mentality is being taken on and defeated. The truth has finally been realised. Ryanair's performance has proven it. Pole vaulting over Aer Lingus in terms of passenger carriage and profitability, but also in terms of customer-focused metrics – its records for on-time departures and protecting customers against loss of luggage are also ahead of rivals – Ryanair proves that competition works. And not just in the short term.

When he started GPA, Ryan generated an economic impact that went far beyond his company. Lacking the scale needed to compete in aerospace manufacturing, Ireland is finding that, in an increasingly sophisticated and diverse global economy, there remain niches of the aerospace industry in which it can compete, including aircraft composites, in-flight entertainment technologies, as well as leasing. From just two companies in the early 1990s, by the autumn of 2007, the Republic is now home to 160 companies involved in the aerospace industry,[12] in no small part thanks to the momentum given to the aircraft leasing business. Unfortunately, and in spite of GPA being originally established in Shannon, most of them are in Dublin.

In August and September of 2007 it seemed as if the view of local interest groups – that their region was unable to compete without state help – was becoming a self-fulfilling prophecy. A string of job losses were announced. August saw 260 jobs go as Analog Devices shed workers in Limerick, and Rothenberger Ireland and Mohawk Europa shed jobs in Shannon. In September, Tyco Electronics announced that a further 178 jobs were to be lost in its manufacturing plant. In all instances, the link with Heathrow was incidental. Those laid off were manufacturing workers with no need to travel

to London in the course of their work. The real cause of the closures –
high labour costs – had its roots in the high cost of doing business
in Ireland.

Local regions are awake to their own interests, but asleep when it
comes to economic reality. They need to wake up. Artificial supports cannot guarantee the location of international business in any
community. In the long run, only a deeply ingrained competitiveness – stemming from high productivity – can do that. But government isn't off the hook. It is important not to give regional interests
what they want; but it is vital to give them what they need.

CHAPTER 9

Planes, Trains and Automobiles

Such an option was rejected at an early stage because it would have involved demolishing six houses which were built on the line.

Irish Times report, summer 2007*

ONLY IN IRELAND

If the new suburbs of Ireland's only metropolis were connected by decent transport, its inverted growth might not be so bad. Few areas have borne the failure of public policy more heavily than our transport system. The quality of urban bus services is universally accepted as being totally out of kilter with the needs of a modern economy. Ten years after it was promised, Ireland's main airport is still without a second terminal. The terminal it has – a legacy of decades of state-run culture – is a place where the time it takes to queue and check-in can often exceed the scheduled time for a flight. There are too few check-in desks and too few car parking spaces, and those that exist cost an arm and a leg.

Ireland's cities are unconnected by motorways; its rail services – with the exception of routes between Dublin and Belfast, Galway and Cork – are laughable. The one decent stretch of motorway, the M50, was expected to carry 40,000 vehicles a day by 2020, but

---

* On why the Harcourt Street–Bray route, already in existence but dormant since 1854, could not be re-opened to cater for a growing population.

97

now carries 100,000. The state's failure to increase capacity in the public transport system contrasts with Ryanair's rapid increase in passengers, from 5,000 in its first year to an estimated 52 million passengers in 2006.

In the long run, the key failure of transport policy stems from the failure to recognise the interplay between spatial strategy and transport policy. Linking key cities to each other by motorway and efficient rail services is a key priority. Linking key cities with their immediate hinterlands is another. Having been exiled to the pub-less hinterlands of the city, proper public transport would spare young couples the long commutes, huge taxi bills and the disruption of contact with family and friends. The impetus towards community living remains strong and there is evidence to suggest that the social implications of this disruption of Ireland's boom are not as bad as many commentators have made out.[1] But the situation is far from perfect.

It looks as if at last a serious effort will be made to redress these deficiencies with the latest National Development Plan (NDP).[2] The plan commits €183 billion in investment over a six-year period. But its time horizon, 2007 to 2013, is too close to the five-year political cycle for comfort; the plan was announced in the run up to the 2007 general election. The opportunity to stress its electoral aspects was not lost with the NDP being billed as an 'investment of €184 billion over the next seven years'. Size, rather than focus and precision, seems to be the main concern. For instance, by covering social infrastructure and social inclusion in its remit – rather than dealing with these goals in another policy plan – the NDP suffers from the same sprawl it aims to cure. Less than one-third of the resources it identifies, some €54.7 billion, actually go towards national development in the truest sense – spending on economic infrastructure.

Having a small number of highly populated cities makes transport policy simpler. The challenge is to provide good public transport within those cities and excellent motorways and rail links between them. With a large number of poorly populated towns, things get complex. Automatically, the fixed cost element of transport infrastructure – train stations, motorway flyovers and bus stations – is multiplied, while the revenue element – the number of taxpayers or paying users in the vicinity of the infrastructure – is reduced. In Ireland today, transport policy is buttered far too thinly to be efficient.

To get the best return for a growing population, future investment also needs to be directed towards areas that will stimulate most economic growth and be most used. The present NDP is a good start. It does recognise the importance of urbanisation, noting that areas of strong population growth have 'helped them to attain a critical mass in terms of population, which supports investment in necessary infrastructure, attracts or generates employment and sustains investment'. The evidence for the assertion is strong.

Against the trend of a stagnating urban population, the population of Dundrum-Sandyford – a suburb of Dublin served by a new suburban tram line – rose by 20.2 per cent between 2002 and 2006.[3] Clonskeagh, Stillorgan and other areas served by the line were also amongst the few of Dublin's southside suburbs to register any increase. Compared to some 25 million annual passengers forecasted to use the Luas line in 2007, the actual number reached 29.5 million,[4] 18 per cent above forecast and way above the city's population growth.

But though not blind to the density issue, the NDP is ambiguous about it. Like the Spatial Strategy, it qualifies the benefits of raising a town's population to 'the wider rural hinterland'. The NDP will devote €11.5[5] billion towards the provision of suburban rail in and around Dublin. It is the largest single investment project in the history of the state and – at the time of writing – the signs so far are that a significant portion of it will be misdirected. On 6 June 2007 – three weeks before election day – the Minister for Transport in the outgoing government announced that the Luas line would be extended from Cherrywood to Bray, Ireland's eighth largest town and home to 30,000 people. But instead of using the most efficient route – the part of the Harcourt Street–Bray line not already used for the Luas – it was proposed to send the new line out to terminate in Fassaroe, a place earmarked for major development.

The reason given for not using the existing dormant infrastructure was that, since its construction by William Dargan[6] in 1854, six houses had been built on the line. In any other country, those houses would have been the subject of a compulsory purchase order. Due to outdated conceptions of land law, the Rail Procurement Agency (RPA), which is responsible for managing expenditure on the project, had been sued by the owners of a listed house near Glencairn. The new route was planned to add thirteen million passenger journeys a year. For the sake of six home owners, the cost of delivering those thirteen million passenger journeys is now significantly higher, and the time for implementing the plan is significantly longer.

Worse still, the chosen line is to an undeveloped area west of the town. By not terminating in Bray – which would have allowed a link up with the DART[7] and rail services to Wicklow, Wexford and Waterford – the project greatly diminishes its own social and commercial return. A chance to help house buyers banished from Dublin to the south-east by house prices is frustrated by a bad approach to transport planning, created in turn by an obsession with residential property.

On the other side of the city, the same thing is happening. Metro North, the plan to connect the north County Dublin town of Swords with St. Stephen's Green, is being given priority as a stand alone project. This is instead of giving priority to a plan that integrates the structures already there. Dublin's disparate transport system consists of a DART line running along the city's eastern coast, two Luas lines through the middle and west of the southern part of the city, and a line from the north city centre reaching north-eastwards, serving neighbouring County Meath and beyond. With no intergrated ticketing or connection between these lines, Dublin is one of Europe's few capitals to lack a proper urban rail service.

Again, densifying urban populations is the solution. The cost benefit analysis of any urban rail system depends on the number of potential users living in its catchment area. The more densely populated Dublin and other cities destined for public transport investment become, the more massive costs like these can be spread over more commuters, reducing the net cost to the taxpayer. As well as the obvious increase in spatial efficiency, proper urban transport is the only answer to Ireland's increasing carbon footprint.

But, in Dublin's case, its official city limits – the area where suburban rail services are concentrated – is one of the few parts of the country where the population is falling, thanks to poor urban planning and high house prices. With the state's population heading for at least five million by 2020 and rising rapidly, this isn't good enough anymore.

Finishing the primary and secondary roads programmes are also key priorities. A core economic objective needs to be to insulate small towns from localised shocks arising from the closure of a major employer. The closure of a factory in Mallow, for example, matters far less if Cork City is twenty minutes away by autobahn than if Cork City is an hour's congested drive away. Properly hooking up main cities with their economic hinterlands won't in itself create a density dividend; but it will help to overcome the worst effects of recent sprawl. By putting residential centres within easier reach of employment centres, houses outside urban areas will become more attractive in relative terms than those within them. As well as cooling huge house price inflation in Ireland's major towns,[8] this will help to cushion the impact that the closure of a major factory in a small town might have on house prices in that town.

If physical connectivity is important, then so is virtual connectivity. In Northern Ireland, the state tendered for the provision of 100 per cent broadband access, allowing full freedom to the firm that eventually won the tender to apply whatever mix of technology was needed. From 50 per cent of households in 2003, availability rose to 100 per cent by the end of 2005, with even Rathlin Island off the coast of Antrim having access. From 10,000 subscribers in 2003, over 160,000 subscribers were recorded by 2006. Achieving the equivalent result within a similarly short space of time should have priority in the Republic. The present NDP devotes twice as much money to the questionable policy of decentralisation as it does to broadband.

BROADER THINKING

With activity in the construction sector slowing down, the NDP is going to cushion at least some of the effects of this on employment. As of August 2007, employment in the sector is falling by over 2 per cent a year. With 280,000 employed in the sector, this represents a rate of job losses of at least 5,000 per month. Given its sheer size, the NDP can absorb a chunk of this. But the ESRI has commented on the plan that that same size – a spend of around €180 billion over a seven year period – will lead to inflation.[9] According to this thinking, though the ESRI are right in principle on this point, their remedy – scaling back the size of the NDP – is flawed. The NDP must be given absolute priority. If, as they might, inflationary threats arise, then current government expenditure should bear the brunt of adjustment. Having risen by 25 per cent between 2004 and 2006 – a rise drowning the size of the public capital budget – current spending growth and the tax burden it necessitates has become a serious threat to the future welfare of the country.

On one other count, the ESRI's assessment of the NDP is simply mistaken. In its assessment of the NDP's approach to rail, the ESRI looks at measures of GDP per capita according to the length of railway network. They conclude that the causal link is negative, not worth pursuing. But the studies cited by the ESRI focus on the UK where population growth has been relatively low for decades. Ireland's experience with the Luas has shown how good rail links can influence people's choices about where to live. The construction of high speed rail as developed in France and Japan would put most Irish towns and cities within less than an hour of each other.

Just as the greater ease of travel between nations is encouraging international migration, so a greater ease of intercity transport makes migration to another city less daunting. High speed rail would encourage more citizens to see the entire country, rather than Dublin, as their oyster. Putting more parts of the country within reach of each other might also help to create something that every Republic should aspire to – a more united and cohesive citizenry.

If only it was that simple. Like any attempt to improve the national condition, the NDP is being held back by a ball and chain that has hung around our necks for centuries: the legacy of land.

CHAPTER 10

The Legacy of Land

Bull McCabe: *There's another law stronger than the common law.*

Father Doran: *What's that?*

Bull McCabe: *The law of the land.*

John B. Keane, *The Field*

It is not too much to say that our entire economy will stand or fall by the use made of the land.

Erskine Childers, 1957

AN OLD DISEASE

The famine is a nineteenth century ghost we have put behind us. Not so one of its strongest by-products: our obsession with land. If we are to house anything between six and nine million people by 2050 in an efficient, productive economy, the ghost of Bull McCabe has to be laid to rest, along with the famine dead.

In many ways, it survives to haunt us today and – second perhaps to an oil price shock – remains the single greatest threat to our new found prosperity. It is also a barrier to the future. Its root causes – the struggle for sheer survival and the memory of it imparted down the generations – are long gone, leaving behind a patchwork structure of land plots in the west of Ireland. But the bee-hive pattern of little fields along the west are more than a reminder of the past.

Terence Dooley recorded how, for most of the last century and before, the possession of land was not just a matter of survival, but also an indicator of social status.[1] In 1964, in his play *The Field*, John B. Keane immortalised the obsession with land in the character of Bull McCabe, a farmer whose obsession with a piece of property drives him to murder, insanity and the destruction of his family. A comment on the extremes to which this obsession could go in individuals, the play could also serve as an ominous warning on how land is being used and planned collectively by the nation.

NEW SYMPTOMS

As the government struggled to complete the National Roads Programme launched under the NDP 2000–2006, the cost of the obsession was becoming horribly clear. In 2004, the Comptroller and Auditor General (C&AG) reported to a shocked nation that the cost of a proposed investment on national road development planned over the period of the NDP, initially put at €7 billion,[2] had more than doubled to €16.4 billion. Blamed partly on 'the lack of costing expertise in the National Roads Authority' – which had led to underestimation of the cost in the first place – the overshoot had other significant roots. Changes to the original plan had increased costs, as had higher than expected inflation.

Yet one other cause was singled out for specific mention: in December 2001 an agreement was struck between the Department of the Environment, Heritage and Local Government and the Irish Farmers Association (IFA) covering the compulsory acquisition of agricultural land. Together with the rising cost of land in urban areas this was, the C&AG said, 'instrumental' to the higher cost of completing the programme. The cost of acquiring land accounted for 14 per cent of programme costs, which was at least €2 billion.

The immediate consequence of this, according to the C&AG, was that 'around half of the programme being managed by the NRA would not be delivered by the end of 2006, while just under 30 per cent will not be delivered by the end of 2008.'[3] The longer-term result was that, as Ireland's population grew much faster than expected, roads were being built much more slowly than expected and congestion was increasing exponentially.

As time went by, the bill grew bigger. By 2006, an official of the Department of Transport reported that the share of total roads spending by the state – around €18 billion between 1999 and 2008 – allocated to the purchase of land had risen to 23 per cent.[4] Some €360 million in taxpayers' money was paid for land for road construction in that year alone. Was the farming community really justified in asking for so much money from the taxpayer? The farming sector have already benefited from massive transfers from the EU – over €40 billion between 1973 and 2007.[5] EU price supports to farmers have made food products in the EU amongst the most expensive in the world, while in Ireland food prices are amongst the highest in Europe.

In the absence of any countervailing legislation, a failure to negotiate with the IFA would have disrupted the Roads Programme. The IFA were doing what everyone else in Ireland had to do in that situation: negotiate for the best possible return. In a situation where nice guys finished last, the IFA could claim with some justification that it was fulfilling its mandate on behalf of a majority of its members. The question was whether, in its negotiations with them, the government was doing the same for the taxpayer.

As land prices in the commuter belt climbed to new heights, the planning process itself became affected. In its county development plan for 2007 to 2013, Monaghan County Council decided in its wisdom to rezone enough land in its remit to allow the county population to rise by 182 per cent. But instead of targeting the town of Monaghan, the main urban centre, to achieve critical mass, the rezoned residential land was to be spread across twenty-nine villages around the county. The National Spatial Strategy has already failed to target population growth in key urban areas. But here was failure on a more spectacular level. Here was a county planning to increase its own population in seven years by more than the entire projected increase for the border region up to the year 2020; a county acting in a manner completely inconsistent with the best available information on population growth. Furthermore, instead of targeting zoning where demand for housing – and employment potential – is greatest, the Council plans to spread that population across its land mass like butter on bread. The fact is that Monaghan's roads, and local services – schools and public transport – are more than inadequate to support even the county's existing population. In a long-needed act of sanity, and using his powers under the 2000 Planning Act, Green Party Environment Minister John Gormley rescinded the decision 'in the interests of ensuring the future sustainable development of the county'.[6]

Why had a local county council taken such actions? In all likelihood, they did so because of pressure from local land owners waiting to see the value of their land increase. As happens so often in Ireland, local and short-term interests are at war with the national long-term interest. On this occasion, the ghost of Bull McCabe was exorcised by a minister's vigilance and determination. But for how long? Should insulating rural Ireland from the chaos of unplanned development be dependent on the discretion of a minister, or should we finally tackle the root cause of bad planning in rural Ireland?

An extreme answer to these problems would be to cap the price of land for new housing development in the commuter belt. Long accepted in Thatcherite Britain, the idea was contemplated by the government in 2002. It had even been proposed by the Labour Party in 2003, only to be rejected. The constitutional guarantee of the right to property can be invoked to strike down any legislation capping the price of land. Introduced in 1937 as totalitarianism was spreading throughout Europe, the guarantee made it difficult for any leftist government to undermine capitalism. Seventy years later it is acting to undermine capitalism in its own way, by driving house prices and road building costs through the roof. Those with valid interests in keeping the price of land uncapped point out that market forces are usually a guarantee of efficient outcomes. Those capable of putting the land to best use would pay the most for it so, in order to allocate land to its best use, its price needs to be able to move up or down accordingly. There is just one problem with this way of thinking.

ECONOMICS 101

The ancient Greeks believed that all things were made from four ingredients: fire, air, water and earth. Economists have always – and still do – believed that everything in the economy is made from four basic ingredients, and the first thing that any economics student does is learn about these four factors of production: enterprise, capital, labour and land.

Like the earth it describes, land is a physical substance yielding everything from oil and minerals to crops and scenery. But it also does one thing more: it defines a space on which economic activity – be it production or consumption – happens. The cost of that space in Ireland today is the biggest driver of rising living costs and falling competitiveness internationally. Land on its own is valueless. Like fire, air and water acting on the earth, enterprise, capital and labour are the things that release the value added from land.

In the first decade of the new millennium, Ireland redefined economics and, by the looks of it, threw ancient Greek wisdom by the wayside. To the outside economic observer, land and property are all that matters. By 2004 – before the house price inflation surge of 2005 and 2006 – the cost of housing in Ireland was one-tenth more expensive than in Paris, one-fifth more expensive than in London, Stockholm or Helsinki and almost twice as expensive as in Berlin or Amsterdam.

Behind rising house prices is the rising price of land. Even in remote Glendalough – miles from any dense urban settlement – the state was, by 2007, paying nearly €2 million for nineteen hectares of land, almost €36,170 an acre and over three times the agricultural value of land. Had the state been driven by market forces – a desire to get the best value for money – the arguments against any control of land prices might have been justified. But some of the prices paid for land by the Roads Programme are determined not by free market thinking, but by negotiations with a politically powerful lobby, the IFA. Similarly, it was hard to understand why €200,000 was paid for each acre of a 150 acre site – some €30 million in all – at Thornton Hall in North County Dublin. The amount paid by the government was not to build luxury apartments, but to resite Dublin's Mountjoy Prison, which is being moved from its original location. The price was around ten times the agricultural value of the land and four times the €26,000 paid per acre for land four miles away in Ratoath. A modestly higher price than the latter would have represented a fair compromise between the natural desire of landowners to get more than agricultural prices and the needs of taxpayers and homeowners to get value for money for road building and house purchases, respectively. But instead of compromise, the balance of the bargain for land purchase continues to be weighed heavily in favour of Bull McCabe, with devastating consequences for the economy.

In 2006 and in response to a question from then Green Party leader Trevor Sargent, Bertie Ahern indicated support for controlling the price of building land. More than that, he was prepared to go the whole hog and deal with any constitutional challenge that might arise if any resultant legislation was challenged: 'If that is the case, then we would have to have a constitutional referendum, which I would also be in favour of.'[7] Three years earlier, Minister of State for Housing and brother of the Taoiseach, Mr Noel Ahern, said the government was examining such a referendum as a way of controlling land costs.[8]

By 2007, Bertie Ahern and Noel Ahern were not only back in government, but they were joined by the Green Party. At the time of writing, there is no sign of movement on this issue.

'BUNGALOW BLISS'

Some more forgivable variants of Bull McCabe syndrome are, ironically, more deadly. If seen from a satellite a hundred miles above the earth, Ireland's population growth would show up as hundreds of little blotches. Seen closer, from an aeroplane perhaps, even the blotches have blotches. The already huge inefficiencies caused by a weak spatial strategy is being made worse by one-off housing.

In the 1980s, the term 'bungalow bliss' was used to describe the growing phenomenon of houses being built in isolated areas disconnected from structured roads. When linked to farming activity, such housing was a natural part of a beautiful rural landscape. Whatever the reasons for this trend, the Irish rural landscape was to witness an outburst of hacienda porches, bay windows and garden gnomes as one-off houses bred like rabbits across the countryside.

Instead of focusing on the merits or demerits of the case for and against one-off housing, the debate has been distorted by a deep cultural fault line running through Ireland, pitching east against west, urbanite against rural dweller. In rural Ireland some feel that restrictions on one-off housing is an attack on their way of life, an attack mounted by the urban elites of the east coast, people whose contempt for rural values is barely disguised. There is some truth here, but not much. The strongest case against one-off housing is not the distaste for Dublin intellectuals, but the way the phenomenon is holding back the social and economic development of the west.

Unfortunately, long-term economic thinking is a million miles away from a debate that arouses deep passions. Opposition to one-off housing tends to come from Dubliners who are upset at its impact on the landscape they enjoy on holidays, with little thought of the valid needs of an area's local economy. It's an approach that is bound to prompt resentment. Minister for Rural, Community and Gaeltacht Affairs and public representative for the Galway West constituency, Éamon Ó Cuív, put it like this: 'Surely if the culture of rural areas is to be preserved, then people from the countryside should not be routinely denied the opportunity to build a family home in their place of origin?'[9]

Anyone in the west has a right to be concerned about their culture being under attack. The Gaeltacht – the area where Irish is spoken regularly – is under siege. Refugees from Galway City's rising property prices seek refuge along the roads west out of the city. On the face of it, the number living in the Gaeltacht is rising. So is the number within it actually speaking Irish. But at 64,265 people, the number of Irish speaking Irish people in 2006 was already outnumbered by the number of UK residents living and working in the country.[10] Far from protecting it, one-off housing is deeply damaging to the west. Apart from inadequate tuition in primary school, if anything is killing the Irish language it is the failure to develop well-clustered towns where Irish speakers can communicate socially and commercially through Irish.

Ó Cuív is not the only one using cultural arguments in favour of one-off housing. Referring in 2005 to Ireland's ancient heritage, then Minister for the Environment and representative for Wicklow, Dick Roche, said: 'We have a dispersed pattern of settlement going back thousands of years.'[11] Professor Seamus Caulfield, retired professor of Archaeology at UCD and member of the Council for the West, contrasted Irish rural settlement patterns in use since the Stone Age with what he dismissively referred to as 'Anglo-Saxon planning models'.[12] The traditional Irish approach to settlement was not to live in towns, but to spread people in diffuse and sporadic patterns. By the 'Anglo-Saxon planning models' Caulfield was presumably referring to the tendency of the English to own larger farms, or to live in properly clustered villages or small towns. Another TD, Johnny Brady, likened An Taisce's refusal to grant permission to some one-off housing applicants to the British Landlords evicting tenants in the nineteenth century.[13]

A century after the land reforms of the nineteenth century eventually undid Cromwell's legacy, it is still warping our thinking about land. It may have been introduced to Ireland by the Anglo-Saxons, but the idea of properly planned rural towns and villages is also a successful feature of most functional countries in Europe. Is the fact that our one-time oppressors are doing something a good enough reason for us to do the opposite, even if this is not to our benefit?

On the other hand there was and remains a serious problem with the failure of those opposed to one-off housing to listen. An Taisce's mindset is too Dublin-centric to be credible to many people in the west. If Bull McCabe was alive and as self-destructive as ever, he would have good reason to be: his critics didn't have a good word to say about him. *Irish Times* columnist Fintan O'Toole is an example of someone perceived to oppose unplanned development in rural Ireland. But he is also, rightly or wrongly, associated with an antipathy to other aspects of rural Ireland – adherence to the Catholic Church and to Irish nationalism – that greatly colours how what he and others like him have to say on planning is received in the west.

In one respect, though, Professor Caulfield was certainly right: one-off development is consistent with the Stone Age, and that is where it is bringing our economy. The truth is that, while the cultural benefits of one-off housing are illusory, the economic costs to the nation and its future are huge. Roche was nearly right when he said, 'The most important ingredient in rural development is population.'[14] But the success of rural development depends on how well it is planned and executed. As Minister Roche was to discover to his own cost, one-off housing has caused serious problems for the delivery of local water services and other services without which no region can develop effectively.

CAUSES, CRISIS, CONSEQUENCES

The chickens came home to roost. Polluted by sewage, Galway City's water supply became undrinkable in March 2007. As usual, the planners and managers who might have planned or prevented the eventually were not called to account. The only political victim of the nine month crisis was Minister Roche, who lost his ministerial position after the 2007 election.[15] The crisis grabbed headlines. But – despite a general election campaign – a comprehensive debate on the way we want to live didn't follow. Thousands of septic tanks and group water schemes are driving up the costs of water supply and sewage, and are increasing the risks of system breakdown and poisoning. The west's fragmented population distribution is making everything difficult. Industry – medical supplies and information technology companies in particular – is taking root in Galway City. But tourist property buyers have driven up the price of property to astronomical levels. For the city's ordinary citizens, the cost of accommodation is a nightmare. Bad public transport – thin population distribution makes it hard to break even on any route around or out of the city – makes life more difficult for those exiled to the city's satellite towns. Galway County typifies the problems of the west. Highly car dependent, it has an ever-increasing carbon footprint. Its sprawling population makes the provision of decent ambulance services or broadband expensive.

The citizens of the west cannot be blamed for demanding the same level of services that exists in the rest of the country. But the structure and distribution of housing in the west makes the provision of most public services – health, electricity, transport, telecommunication, water supply, sewage and education – relatively expensive on a per capita basis compared to more densely packed towns. Even at lower levels of provision in the west, it is quite likely that the average electricity user, the average water consumer and the average bus commuter in Dublin is heavily subsidising his or her counterpart in more remote regions.

We can have a thriving, productive economy with a flourishing population and still live in a country that remains relatively underpopulated, green and pleasant. But, as was argued in Chapter 8, we have choices to make. Compared with almost any other prosperous and moderately populated European country, Ireland's cities and towns contain too few people. Land is not by itself economically productive but is instead a crucial input into activities that are. If we

114

persist in retaining one of the highest costs of land in the developed world, and if our planning system and attitudes to land go unchanged, then the price paid by our economy will be just as high. But if we can realize the full potential of our land – especially in urban areas where it floats in the air above our heads – our economy's competitiveness and the quality of our young peoples' lives can finally start doing justice to our status as a wealthy economy. Striking that bargain relies on getting over the biggest obstacle of all: politics.

CHAPTER 11

Ireland of the Hundred Governments

How can anyone govern a nation that has 246 different kinds of cheese?

President of France Charles de Gaulle

A HOUSE DIVIDED

Urban and spatial planning, the roll out of critical infrastructure and the day-to-day management of simple local services are becoming a comedy of errors. With just 4.2 million souls, Ireland is a land of a hundred governments, each vying with each other for control and each subject to the relentless barrage of local and sectional interest pressures. And yet local authorities, designed around county structures, but often covering areas smaller than a county, have the power to decide their own policy in a host of areas that require national or regional solutions. Transport is an obvious example where this causes projects with cross-county dimensions to get frustrated, delayed or implemented at a drastically higher cost than necessary. In the eternal battle between the national and the tribal wills, the tribes keep winning. Faced with an often irreconcilable mix of local interests, national government departments attempting to govern for the good of the nation are facing mission impossible. Irish policy making is short-term and local, when it needs to be long-term and national.

117

The coordination problem is made worse by the resource problem. Local authorities want to be big boys in local government, designing, building and operating pieces of infrastructure by themselves. As a result, the speed for infrastructure roll-out depends not on how much is needed, but on the resource levels – usually never enough – and speed levels – usually too slow – available to them. Local authorities can appeal to An Bord Pleanála about projects that are not only clearly in the national interest but within their border, which is a good thing, but also about projects in neighbouring counties. If Ireland did not have over a hundred local authorities, this latter right would be confined to projects of national proportions – motorways, for example – where some consultation with local authorities is obviously desirable. The sheer number and small size of local authorities has turned what should be simple transport projects into Byzantine intrigues of local politicking, involving chronic delays and rapidly increasing costs. Relative to local authorities and national transport bodies, central government is often too weak to knock heads together. To achieve proper local planning, Ireland needs local authorities with proper powers, resources and prestige. Unfortunately, this has to come as part of an overall reform of the political system.

In a host of policy areas Ireland is behind the rest of Europe. Is it politicians' fault? Or is there something deeper at work, something paralysing decision making at the highest level in the land?

In most functioning democracies, opposition parties attempt to gain votes from government parties by appealing to popular opinion. That means opposing government policy where it can be proven to be contrary to the public interest. Unlike most other European countries, this isn't working in Ireland. As discussed in Chapter 6, instead of being led by the largest opposition party, Fine Gael, opposition to the Groceries Order was led by consumer evangelist Eddie Hobbs, whose TV programme, *Rip-Off Republic* forced the government to finally implement a reform that had been waiting twenty years. Instead of the opposition championing the cause of commuter-belt drinkers, most Fine Gael and Labour Party TDs stood by and watched as Progressive Democrat Minister Michael McDowell single-handedly tried to push reform through his own government.

Neither would Fine Gael dare to oppose one-off housing, despite the huge damage it is doing: its voter base is too rural. And, while criticising the government's decentralisation plans, Fine Gael made it clear in the 2007 election campaign that it would not reverse the jobs that had already been decentralised. The fear of losing votes in the constituencies that had gained the jobs was just too strong.

On these and other issues, some backbench Fine Gael TDs have stood shoulder to shoulder with some Fianna Fáil backbench TDs in a way that makes it hard to understand why they were not in the same party. Instead of advocating a reform of inefficient local authority structures and planning laws, the opposition were – with the exception of the Green Party – silent on the issue. And when the Shannon-Heathrow issue blew up in 2007, Fine Gael's position was short-termist and opportunistic. In an attempt to win disaffected government voters in the west, it called on the government to do something that Fine Gael itself was unlikely to have done had it won the recent election: use its shareholding in Aer Lingus to prevent the loss of the Heathrow slot. The proposal was not in the region's interest in the long run and, advertising as it did the region's self-proclaimed inability to compete internationally, probably not even in its short-term interest. It certainly wasn't in the nation's long-term interest. So why were Fine Gael going down this road? What they were doing was exposing the latest manifestation of a deadly disease that continues to cripple decision making.

MÉ FÉINERS

One of the surprises of the 2007 election was the poor performance, compared to expectations, of Sinn Féin.[1] Espousing a mix of nationalist politics and left-of-centre economics, the party had been expected to gain seats as an underclass supposedly left behind by the years of prosperity showed its anger. It never happened. One reason might have been the belief that Sinn Féin would harm the economy so much that even the underclass would be worse off. Sinn Féin's performance in the economic debate in that election campaign has been cited as a key reason for its failure to gain seats. But is it possible that a deeper, more entrenched force than Sinn Féin poses an even bigger threat?

Many political scientists have noted that the more sensitive an electoral system is to small swings in voting – that is, the more a 1 percentage change in voting turns into seat changes in parliament – the more politicians have to worry about a certain kind of voter: swing voters. The theory goes like this. There are two types of voters, those who tend to vote for parties regardless of their own interests and those who vote on the basis of what a party does for them. In the lexicon of political economy, the former are called 'ideological' voters. The word used by that same lexicon for the latter is 'swing' voters, but let's call them Mé Féiners.

It certainly looks as if governments of all hues have been thick with the Mé Féiners. Lobby groups from all sectors of the economy seem to have privileged access to government. Unions, farming leaders and big business have no problem bending the ear of ministers. Events like RTÉ's *Rip-Off Ireland* series aside, it seems left to the powerless voter to fume away in a ditch. But is that really the way it is? The reform of the Groceries Order shows that it isn't. The views of ordinary voters can influence policy, for good or ill depending on your point of view, when they really register with politicians. The trouble is that this doesn't seem to happen very often. And where it does, it is to support a localised interest that is often – but not always – contrary not just to the national overall interest but usually to the long-term interest of the locality in question.

Ireland's single transferable vote (STV) electoral system is one of the most sensitive in the world (amongst EU countries, only Malta has a similar system). Allowing voters to vote for multiple candidates in order of choice in multi-seat constituencies leads to a very unique result: a governing party or coalition can lose seats while actually retaining – and in theory even gaining – first preference votes. In 2007, Fianna Fáil received 41 per cent of the vote, entitling it on a pro-rata basis to 69 seats in Ireland's 166-seat Dáil. But a lucky break in transfer votes and good vote management saw it receive seventy-eight seats and return to power, albeit in a multi-party coalition. In theory, however, it is possible for Fianna Fáil – or any major party in government with that profile of votes and seats – to retain the same first preference share, 41 per cent in this case, and lose enough seats to lose power. If you know that – and if you are a Mé Féiner who knows other voters continue voting for the same party they've always supported – that makes you powerful.

In Ireland, strongly vocal and highly self-conscious groups of voters know that the broad mass of other voters – the great majority of voters whose long-term interest would benefit from that reform – would not necessarily reward politicians who sided with them. They might not even notice. Politicians know it too. But they also know that the interest groups would use their vote against or for the government depending on how the government acts. Up to now, asking politicians to engage in serious reform – the kind of reform needed to prepare Ireland for a century of epoch-making growth – is like asking them to commit suicide. The Groceries Order and the reform of taxi licenses were milestones that showed how popular opinion was becoming more powerful. But compared to other even more powerful groups the treatment of the food industry and taxi drivers seems inconsistent at best. At worst, it seems capricious and cynical.

Retail outlets and food manufacturers experienced reductions in margins as a consequence of falling food prices, once the Order was rescinded. And yet they continue to pay huge commercial rents in an unreformed property market, not to mention rapidly rising local authority charges that fund an unreformed system of local government. Taxi drivers saw tens of thousands wiped off the value of their licenses overnight. Some had to remortgage their houses.

And yet every time a taxi driver goes into a pub or pays an electricity bill, he or she faces price levels that are amongst the highest in Europe, price levels caused by state protectionism. If reform is good – and it is – it is good for everyone. Piecemeal reform is unjust; and yet this is what the dynamics of Ireland's political system dictates.

ELECTORAL REFORM

Remarkable and at the same time disturbing, Margaret Thatcher's ability to defeat powerful interests opposed to economic reform was a clear reminder of how differently Irish and British politics work. Thatcher could see off coal miners, hospital workers and public servants with a wave of her handbag. Irish politicians appear to faint at the slightest hint of unrest. Was she a tough and hard-headed woman? Are Irish politicians lily-livered cowards? Or is it simply that, unlike Ireland's, Britain's electoral system allowed Thatcher to make these decisions and get re-elected?

In Britain, a government doesn't need a majority of votes to get elected. In theory, a government with just 30 per cent of the vote can retain a majority of seats in parliament provided it gets the largest single number of votes in more than half the constituencies. In practice, 30 per cent is too low a threshold. But, with the ability in practice to obtain a majority with anything over 36 per cent of the vote, British governments that obtain much higher vote shares have a power that Irish governments can only dream of. Even if a reform measure is bitterly opposed by an organised minority, unless that minority accounts for 2 or 3 per cent of voters, and if the government is not hugely unpopular,[2] it can push through with reform. And that means they can do what Irish governments cannot: govern for the long-term.

Despite warnings of dire consequences for herself and her party, Thatcher pushed through reform after reform between 1979 and 1990, winning three elections in a row. The poll tax[3] was the exception that proved the rule. With her popularity damaged by previous reforms, Thatcher finally proposed a reform that riled a significant number of voters and was toppled. Nonetheless, her long run of aggressive government proved how electoral systems can determine the power of government. In 2007, in spite of fifteen years of prosperity, the Irish government has failed to implement reforms across a whole range of economic sectors, reforms that had been implemented in the UK decades earlier.

But it is not our politicians who are to blame. Introduced into Ireland – but not the UK – by the British early in the last century, Ireland's STV system of Proportional Representation (PR) was designed to ensure that the political passions of the state found political, rather than violent, expression. Such a system gives encouragement to small parties. The British bequeathed a similar system to Israel. As Irish governments grappled with high unemployment and militant trade unions in the 1980s, Israeli President Herzog was presiding over a state where internal disorder was growing. When historian Martin Gilbert wrote of Israel's political system that 'The fragmentation of parties also arose from a national tendency to be disputatious and contentious,'[4] he might just as well have been referring to Ireland. In the 1980s, Herzog was to advocate the adoption of the British two party first-past-the-post system for Israel. Under that system a party merely needs to win more votes than any other party in each constituency to win an election. For example, winning 30 per cent of the vote – less than a third – can elect a party to government provided it wins the highest share of votes in over half of the geographic constituencies.

Whatever about Israel, is this what Ireland needs? Defeating the militant coal mining unions was one thing. But Thatcher's failure to pay attention to the economic decline of England's northern regions, not to mention her neglect of Scotland, puts the British system in perspective. The British government's decision to implement the poll tax in Scotland in advance of doing so in England – using Scotland as a guinea pig – was reminiscent of its fondness for locating nuclear power plants and weapons bases as far away from south-east England as possible.

Germany and Holland have forms of PR that are half way between the extremes of the Irish and British systems. Proportionate in the best sense, their systems prevent excessive dominance by the largest party. But they also limit the ability of minorities or regional interests to hold governments to ransom. Mainly directed at right- and left-wing extremists, Germany's system excludes from representation any party with less than 5 per cent of the vote, unless one of its representatives has a direct mandate. Half of the seats in Germany's Bundestag are filled directly by the political parties from their own lists and according to the share of the vote received. The other half are elected directly from geographical constituencies. It is not a coincidence that these countries have good urban planning, low price services sectors and well-functioning transport systems.

Previous chapters have pointed to vast untapped reservoirs of growth potential for our economy: in public service reform, in well-planned urbanisation, in a proper transport system and in greater competition in the domestic service markets of our economy. All of this is possible. But it is only politically achievable if electoral reform is undertaken first. A system that allows one constituency to hold up government policy – worse still a minority of opinion within that constituency – has had its day. From across Ireland's political divide, former Fianna Fáil Taoiseach Charles Haughey and former Fine Gael leader Garret FitzGerald, at different times in the 1990s, called for Ireland's electoral system to be reformed. Earlier, referenda proposing electoral change were put before the electorate only to be defeated. The fear of unlimited Fianna Fáil government – a likely outcome of such reform in the 1960s – was too strong. Forty years later, coalition government is the norm. The perceived risk of reform has shrunk beneath its need.

If it still frustrates the purist, the pace of political reform has at least gathered pace in recent years. But it remains incomplete and incoherent. No longer able to serve as local authority representatives, TDs have, in theory, been focused on the task of legislating and governing for the nation. In reality, TDs have become substitute local authority representatives. Local authority reform has shifted vast powers to local authority managers, managers that local councilors are powerless to curtail. All politics is local. Few of the major issues facing the country can be addressed properly by politicians who are ignorant of water supply, land rezoning and a host of other issues that local authorities deal with. For a large number of TDs, but not for all, local authorities are good training grounds for politics. Familiarity with local issues in the Dáil needs to be complemented by expertise at national level.

In the 2007 election erstwhile Green Party TD Dan Boyle and erstwhile Progressive Democrat TD Michael McDowell lost their Dáil seats. Fianna Fáil TD Pat Carey very nearly lost his. Labour Senator Derek McDowell never came close to election. The experiences of these men, amongst the more cerebrally capable politicians in the country, begs the question: need direct election by popular vote – a core value of democracy – always mean direct election of the person, or can the democratic will of the electorate also be expressed in favour of the party, allowing that party to choose the person. A good electoral system can have both. Being less seismic and unstable, Germany's PR system has a further advantage over Ireland's: as well as having members elected directly by the people, the Bundestag contains representatives nominated directly by their party.

Another anomaly of Ireland's electoral system is the phenomenon of some citizens having two votes where others have none.[5] Reform of the Seanad to allow for direct election by the people would have further advantages. Nominated by the taoiseach of the day, former Senators John Robb, Mary McAleese and Maurice Hayes were part of a tradition of allowing those born in Northern Ireland to speak in the Oireachtas. An era of closer cooperation between North and South[6] warrants turning a tradition into an entitlement. The representation of Irish emigrants in the Seanad is another overdue reform. However, the suggestion to allow emigrants to vote in the Dáil is a dangerous one. In 1775, Americans revolted against taxation without representation; representation without taxation is just as likely to cause trouble in Ireland. For a growing number of reasons, the technology of political decision making in Ireland is now redundant. In a new century facing massive policy challenges, the time has come for complete and systematic reform.

In another sense, representation without taxation is already a problem in Ireland. Local councilors are forced to provide local services and local presentation, but are denied the ability to raise significant taxes from a broad base of taxpayers. As a consequence, the one sector they can tax – local businesses – pay a cripplingly disproportionate burden. And yet Margaret Thatcher's demise over the poll tax showed just how much resistance there was to any form of local taxation. But was that resistance to local taxation per se? Or was it that those on whom the burden of the poll tax fell felt the overall system of taxation was inequitable. Or was it because they were dissatisfied with the quality of local services, or the fact that the UK was entering a housing slump? Or simply that after a decade of Thatcher's rule, her colleagues were looking for any excuse to get rid of her? At the end of the 1980s, the poll tax became a catalyst rather than a cause of her demise.

Still, systematic and cohesive reform of government is difficult at the best of times. But there are encouraging signs that the electorate is not only increasingly sophisticated, but able to accept the link between good local government and raising revenues. With increasing success, the user-pays principle is being applied by local authorities for bin collection charges, while politicians seeking to gain electoral advantage from opposing this[7] have made little progress. The problem with advocating local taxation at the moment is that, although it exists, its base is not only weak, but unfair. Actually it constitutes a form of slavery whereby local businesses – the slaves of the local government financing system – pay often exorbitant rates in order to fund the services provided to a broader population that makes a much smaller contribution to local authority financing. In its 2007 Programme for Government, Fianna Fáil and the Greens have committed to the concept of directly elected mayors. It is a good reform: strong elected councils with elected city mayors will expose local government to the full rigours of public scrutiny. But with representation must come taxation and this brings other issues clearly into focus.

IRELAND OF THE HUNDRED GOVERNMENTS

From the mists of the nineteenth century, Ireland has inherited twenty-nine county councils, five county boroughs, five borough corporations, forty-nine urban district councils and twenty-six boards of town commissioners. Even the capital city is fragmented: instead of having one unified council, Dublin is managed by four separate local authorities. The sheer number of authorities increases overhead costs, policy duplication and makes the challenge of national policy coordination vastly more difficult than it should be. Consolidating that number would help address another problem with local government: uneven cultures of corporate governance. In 2007, a report by the Committee for Performance Awards (CPA) confirmed that all 274 local authority managers who applied for a performance-related bonus last year received one. Most received between €5,000 and €13,000. Doubtless, many deserved them; but all of them? It was a year in which two counties suffered the contamination of water supply.

A further problem is local authority finance. Leaning too heavily on business rates, local authority financing needs drastic reform. But, as the base of funding is broadened, the top-heavy structures it supports need to narrow. Like a pyramid that is upside-down, local authority structures need to be turned around so that their base – both in terms of financial support and ground level staff – is wider and broader than the officialdom on top. The same could be said about the architecture of governance in the whole country. As well as a national government, Ireland is also governed by regional governments (in theory), local government and a growing number of official but unaccountable organisations.

The highly misnomered BMW (border, midlands and western) region was carved out of the country's north-west half in order to retain access to EU structural funds. Previously designated an 'Objective 1' area because of its low level of GDP per capita, Ireland as a whole has long ceased to justify EU aid, its GDP per capita having surpassed the EU average some time in the late 1990s. To keep the funds coming, the country was – for EU purposes – redesigned to identify a region where GDP per capita was still below the relevant threshold for aid. Apart from this, the division had no governmental structures relating to it. But the two regions of Ireland were given their own assemblies with expenses and limited, ineffective, powers.

In 1994, eight regional authorities were established, authorities with shapes and sizes that, from a planning point of view, are strategically sensible. One of them – Dublin – was an amalgamation of the four local authority areas that filled its county border. In the coming decade, Dublin as an economic entity was to expand up to its county borders and beyond. The regional dimension to government policy is vital. Population and economic growth happens at regional, not local, level. For that reason, the roll out of infrastructure, urban planning and regional policies needs to be coordinated and implemented by a manageable number of powerful authorities covering functional, geographic zones. And yet we also need local authorities. How can duplication between these two structures be avoided?

The case for amalgamating Dublin's four local authorities[8] into an integrated single authority with an elected government was overwhelming. With sufficient powers, a Dublin government could deal with the problems of sprawl, urban planning and transport development that it faces now and in the coming century. The other regions created in 1994 are also well-designed for targeting urbanisation, developing integrated transport systems and rolling out infrastructure. As well as electoral reform, a total revamp of public governance in Ireland is now a priority. One central government with fifteen departments is joined by two aforementioned regional assemblies (there is a strong case for abolishing these), the eight aforementioned regional authorities, and over one hundred local authorities. Heading into the twenty-first century, we are relying on structures of local government invented over a hundred years ago.

In many respects, the eight regional authorities represent the way of the future, not only for the task of regional economic planning but more importantly as enlarged and more efficient local authorities.[9] Governing larger land masses would be consistent with proper transport planning, and improved coordination with bodies such as the National Roads Authority. It would also achieve massive economies of scale arguments. One hundred local authorities governing for 4.2 million people involves massive waste issues in terms of duplicating core staff and building costs, to name just some. Our leading politicians regard local authority reform as impossible. It is not; it is merely the next, as yet untested, frontier of reform. In fact, there is a place where it has been done, a place so critical to the future of this state and its people that the next chapter is devoted to it: Northern Ireland.

PART IV

VISION IN THE DESERT

If you will it, it is no dream.

Theodor Herzl, on the idea of founding
an Israeli state, 1905

CHAPTER 12

A Nation Once Again

As I grow older, I care less and less which flag is flown and which anthem is played where I live.

Sir Kenneth Bloomfield

TRADING PLACES

There was a time when even most of Northern Ireland's Catholics would refuse to contemplate any form of re-unification with the South. For most of the period since the famine, the six counties that make up Northern Ireland performed much better economically. It suffered from the famine and from emigration, but never to the same degree as the South. At its lowest point, the population of the Republic in 1961, 2.8 million, was just 43 per cent of the pre-famine level of the twenty-six counties. Northern Ireland reached its lowest point in 1901, a sign that it was recovering much more quickly; its population that year was 75 per cent of its pre-famine level. By 2002, its population had finally recovered to its pre-famine level. In fact, its population of 1,685,000[1] in 2002 exceeded the 1,648,900 level recorded in 1841. In the same year, the Republic was still over two million under its 1841 level.

From being the most prosperous part of the island in the nineteenth and twentieth century, Northern Ireland's GDP per capita is now lower than that of the Republic. It remains the United Kingdom's poorest region. Lacking the scale of Asian rivals, Northern Ireland's heavy engineering and shipbuilding companies cannot survive the twin challenges of growing competition and technological change. Untrammeled by an industrial legacy, the South's economy tuned into the post-industrial growth of a globalised world, helped greatly by strong multinational investment and participation in the euro.

Until recently, both the Republic of Ireland and Northern Ireland were economically dependent. The Republic received massive transfers from the EU, from common agricultural policy (CAP) related payments in the 1970s and 1980s and from EU structural and cohesion funds in the 1990s. But while the Republic has shaken off this dependency – it will soon become a net contributor to the EU – Northern Ireland continues to rely on subvention from the UK. However its unemployment rate, around 5 per cent, is close to that of the Republic and its retail sector is booming, reflecting an economy over 60 per cent of which is dependent on state support. In an echo of the Republic fifty years ago, Northern Irish business people complain that young people see lucrative potential careers only in the civil service, medicine or outside Northern Ireland.[2] Emotional or historical arguments aside, probably the strongest case against reunification with the South was put by the then deputy leader of the Ulster Unionist Party, John Taylor, in 1997: at £4 billion sterling, the size of the British government's annual stipend to the North's economy was something the Republic couldn't afford.

But events, and history, have taken a turn. Although now €9 billion, Northern Ireland's subvention is less than the Republic's annual expenditure on capital infrastructure, estimated to reach €10.2 billion in 2007.[3] If there are economic arguments against reunification, this isn't one of them. More interesting still is the prospect that, by pooling economic resources, the North and South could realize economies of scale, and grow at a faster rate together than they can alone.

Another twist was that, by 2006, John Taylor – no longer a Unionist politician[4] – was proprietor of Alpha Group and had taken ownership of several local newspapers in the Republic. Far from a unionist infiltration of the Republic, Taylor's sentiments were nationalist, if only economically: 'When it comes to the media, I may be a unionist, but I am more of a nationalist. I am trying to keep them here in Ireland.' The rich irony was that Alpha's southern operations were headquartered in Birr in County Offaly, where Taylor is reported to frequent.[5] The Irish government is trying to move unwilling civil servants into Birr in an effort to bring public sector jobs to the area that should arguably be located in the capital.[6] It takes an Ulster Unionist to bring the kind of meaningful and sustainable economic activity that the town actually needs.

A frequent complaint of British politicians about Ireland in the nineteenth century was that, by the time someone had come up with an answer to the Irish Question, the Irish had changed the question. From asking whether reunification is possible, the question to be asked might instead be this one: what kind of unity *is* both acceptable and possible?

CHANGING THE QUESTION

Throughout the late 1990s and early 2000s, the OECD, the International Monetary Fund (IMF) and even the European Central Bank were singing the praises of the Republic's economic performance. By 2006, even the Shadow Chancellor of the UK's Conservative Party George Osborne was paying tribute to the Republic and advocating that the UK should follow the Republic's example.[7] Through their fingers at first but in an increasingly open way, business people in Northern Ireland are beginning to look to the Republic for inspiration. Worried about public sector dominance, influential business people in the North got together to form a task force to chart out the North's economic future.[8] The issues of the long-term decline of manufacturing, particularly in Belfast, and the dominance of the public sector in the North's economy were on its agenda. Economic re-unification with the South was definitely not.

But the case for lowering the North's corporation tax rate, an objective shared across the political spectrum, was increasingly made with reference to the South. As task force Chairman Sir George Quigley put it: 'The Republic's share of manufacturing output in the European Union increased by some 150 per cent in the 1990s. The broadly comparable figure for Northern Ireland was 33.3 per cent.' The task force's document was careful to note that any tax change 'would of course be a matter for the UK government'. But the open expression of the idea of the Republic as an example to follow is a landmark development.

The comparison goes beyond corporation tax. Although the North's unemployment rate is not much higher than the South's – and among the lowest in the UK – employment levels there tell a very different story. In the Republic half the population – some 2.1 million people – are now at work. In the North only 40 per cent – some 780,000 – are at work, a large share of them in state employment. The difference partly reflects the South's younger age profile. But it also reflects a large and unsustainable number of people in Northern Ireland who are classified as 'economically inactive'.

If inroads are to be made here, taxes in Northern Ireland need to fall. That much is understood across the religious divide. What is less understood is that they need not only to fall below where they are now, but they need to fall below – and remain below – the levels prevailing in the UK. Like the Republic of Ireland, Northern Ireland finds itself on the periphery of the European land mass, one of the factors contributing to the decline in the North's industrial base in the last century. Although no longer enough, in overcoming a God-given handicap, the Republic's relatively lower corporation tax rates has given its economy a critical kick start.

Other aspects of the Republic's political economy have helped. The Republic's participation in the euro, leading to interest rates significantly lower than UK averages and a common exchange rate with most of continental Europe, puts in focus one of the major difficulties holding back foreign direct investment in the North. As well as hampering FDI in the North, the different currency and taxation regimes North and South – on top of the North's higher interest rates – have held back a region that needs a boost. The area of the country worst affected by this cleavage is Donegal. Part of both Ulster and the Republic, most of Donegal's land mass faces a different monetary and tax regime, a key reason why it remains Ireland's poorest county.

Resolving this does not require re-unification in a traditional sense. If Northern Ireland had a right to print its own bank notes, it could form a monetary authority that could participate in Ireland's Central Bank within the European Central Bank. Just as monarchist Spain and republican France share a common currency, so could the North and South of Ireland.

Northern Ireland needs independence from Westminster in terms of economic management. It also needs close economic integration with the South, as joint investment programmes agreed between the UK government, the Republic and the Northern Ireland executive recognise. It also shares problems relating to the provision of public services with the Republic: the high costs of providing electricity, water and gas, to mention a few. These problems can only be addressed by pooling the populations of North and South to reduce the per-person cost of these services. Unlike the Republic, the North's ability to solve this problem, even with devolution, is limited. The capacity for both North and South to together create an all-island economy with a common currency and tax platform and an integrated market for utilities, is exciting. In autumn 2007, there are plans to integrate the electricity market on the island. It's a process with much further to go, but not before the legacy of history is addressed.

In 2007, addressing the Merriman School – one of the Republic's regular public think tanks – unionist Sir Kenneth Bloomfield said the idea of Irish re-unification was not unthinkable. The statement was significant on two counts. Sir Kenneth had been secretary to the Sunningdale Government, a short-lived and failed attempt made in 1974 to build a government that shared power between Catholics and Protestants. If that failure was tragic, the other was a blessing. In November 1988, Sir Kenneth survived an attempted assassination by the Irish Republican Army (IRA). While he wasn't advocating a united Ireland, his comments illustrated that something unexpected was happening. The decommissioning of its weapons by the IRA and the referendum decision by the Republic's voters to seek unity by means of persuasion rather than a constitutional claim on Northern Ireland have not, as some predicted, reduced the likelihood of a united Ireland. Together with rapid economic change, they are increasing it.

Sir Kenneth's hint came with a warning: 'Please do not suppose that if, in some future poll, 50.1 per cent of the electorate were to vote for Irish unity, the outvoted 49.9 per cent would tramp into the new jurisdiction like a defeated army.' The reality is, for a majority of unionists, the imagery of Irish re-unification – one of defeat – is a psychological obstacle to achieving the huge economic benefits. But today's world is one in which sovereignty is being rapidly redefined. The EU, the Eurozone, the UN and the World Trade Organisation are examples of how nation states pool and trade their sovereignty in different ways. As practical business people and politicians try to reconcile the differing emotions of their constituents, any consensus on re-unification is going to have to de-emphasise its cultural aspects and instead strongly emphasise the mutual gains.

In November 2005, Northern Ireland Secretary Peter Hain cut the number of local authorities in Northern Ireland from twenty-eight down to seven. Put together, his reforms would see the total number of local authority bodies – authorities as well as councils – fall from sixty-seven to twenty. The following March, Hain announced that the number of public bodies would fall from 154 to 75. More than just cutting overheads and bureaucracy, the reforms were aimed at improving the effective design of government in the six northern counties of the island. For some, they were too severe and their sudden implementation contrasted with the more consensus-minded way of doing things south of the border. But if they were too severe then at least Hain's reforms were what they claimed to be – proper reforms. As mentioned, the North is also several years ahead of the Republic in broadband accessibility.

As well as the unification of the electricity market,[9] infrastructural investment in the North is now being co-funded by the South. Cross migration between North and South is increasing and in 2007, for the first time, KPMG – an accountancy and consultancy firm – produced all-island accounts for its financial performance. KPMG's headquarters on Dublin's Harcourt Street are, ironically, directly across the road from the house in which the founder of modern Unionism Edward Carson was born.

Would Carson be turning in his grave? Re-unification does not involve the economic annexation of the North by the South, but a merger of equal and opposite advantages. On one end of the island is a low-tax dynamic economy with a growing population and a state that is smaller than the private sector which funds it. On the other is an economy with a low cost base, a good culture of political decision making, and systems of local government, and land and urban planning that are better than in the South. If the Republic and the North were two companies, the case for a merger would be overwhelming. But they are not; they are historic and political entities with identities and memories.

HOPE AND HISTORY

Although he cared less and less what flag was flown, Sir Kenneth Bloomfield doesn't yet speak for all Protestants. A little over a month after his address to the Merriman School, Ulster Bank Group Chairman Alan Gillespie tested the waters on who did by calling for a merger between the Republic's Industrial Development Authority (IDA) and Northern Ireland's Invest Northern Ireland. Nigel Dodds, a minister in the North's power-sharing executive, responded by describing the proposal as 'interesting'. But only a few days later the same executive's Finance Minister Peter Robinson rejected the move: 'I am not going to hide the fact there would be major political issues involved,' he said.[10] At least where Ireland is concerned, Marx was right: the burden of history does weigh like a nightmare on the brain of the living.

But if unionists raise the prospect of re-unificaiton in less than hostile terms, the appropriate response from the South is that re-unification is not what is at issue. What is at issue is far less threatening. Regardless of what flag is flown or anthem is sung in its respective parts, both the North and South of Ireland will eventually have to accept the case for economic reunification as being completely separate from political reunification. Unless, that is, Ulster is to remain in a state of permanent economic supplication.

CHAPTER 13

Once Again a Nation

His father's from Fermanagh, his mother's from Fiji, neither a hurling stronghold.

Mícheál Ó Muircheartaigh on hurling star
Seán Óg Ó hAilpín

A HIDEOUS CHASM

During the famine *The Times* in London warned that future Irish prosperity would be based on a 'hideous chasm'.[1] In the century that followed the famine, a once teeming country became a ghostly shadow of itself. And if it was an attraction to tourists, Ireland's underpopulated countryside was also a symbol of the cultural emaciation that accompanied the emigration of millions people. As its most Celtic and distinctive parts were depopulated, Ireland became Leinsterised and Anglicised.

Those of a utilitarian bent justified the famine by pointing out the increase in average incomes that would result. According to this view, the greater prosperity of the minority left behind justified the death or departure of the majority. But the economist Thomas Malthus argued that famine in Ireland was nature's way; such was the brutal mentality of the age of *laissez-faire* and *laissez-mourir*.[2] In the last century the totalitarian regimes of Europe and Asia brought this logic to a more activist and grotesque conclusion.

In this century the battle between materialism and humanity has been gradually replaced by another battle between materialism and culture. Ever present, those of a utilitarian bent transferred their arguments from people to culture, arguing in the 1960s that the Irish language was an impediment to economic progress. More recently, the Fine Gael Party argued that Irish language lessons should no longer be compulsory for secondary school students. Its main motive was to gain votes amongst parents who feel that having to learn their own language would impede their offsprings' abilities to gain points for prize university courses in the Leaving Certificate. By 2007, one in eight students is dropping out of Irish in the Junior Certificate.[3] One can hardly blame the parents, who are under severe pressure to give their offspring the best possible start economically. In fairness, Fine Gael's proposal was accompanied by others aimed at tackling the real problem with Irish learning: its woeful inadequacy at primary school level.

But the proposal came at a point when the whole basis of gaining points in the Leaving Certificate was being questioned in favour of more directly meritocratic and effective criteria for university courses (interest in the course, for example). Moreover, it reflected an unpatriotic and lazy mentality of cultural defeatism in Ireland; one that always favours selling off our cultural heirlooms as a substitute for the hard work needed to build long-term prosperity. The residue of a national inferiority complex and a form of cultural self-hatred, it's a mentality that is causing us to silently abandon who we are at a time when prosperity and confidence makes us more able to assert it.

Even if it was necessary, the sacrifice of one's own culture isn't a price worth paying for economic prosperity. But as Sweden, Denmark and Finland have shown, it isn't necessary. These countries have retained their cultural identity, raised their offspring to learn excellent English, and have still managed to build a competitive advantage – one based on research, innovation and hard work – that far exceeds our own. Israel built its economy and revived its culture more or less at the same time. Having failed to protect her cultural

identity, Ireland is still struggling to develop indigenous high technology industry.

As well as the enemy within, Irish culture faces an awesome
adversary without. Although hugely benign as far as its economic
implications go, globalisation's cultural impact on threatened
cultures has been so far negative. The huge investment needed to
sustain any mass media outlet makes it difficult for the private
sector to broadcast in minority languages. The sheer size of the
world's dominant mass media outlets – mostly Anglo-American
and English based – exerts a huge gravitational pull on the world,
helping to kill more and more of the world's indigenous languages.[4] Despite this, some 1.7 million people in Ireland are, as of
2007, capable of speaking Irish.[5] Up slightly from 1.57 million in
2002, the figure suggests that Irish speaking is, so far, holding its
own. But a deluge of immigration could wipe it off the linguistic
map forever.

The core problem facing Irish is the few opportunities to speak it.
Languages ultimately survive by being used in networked communities in which a sufficient number of people within a short enough
distance of each other speak the language. In Ireland today such networked communities are few and far between. Like a glacier, the
physical Gaeltacht – a collection of small Irish speaking areas dot-
ted mostly around the west of Ireland – is receding to the western
fringes of the country. The number of Irish speakers using the language everyday in the Irish speaking regions – about 63,000 – is
already outnumbered three to one by the number of immigrants
from the EU in the country.[6] The Irish-speaking share of the population in the Gaeltacht area has declined since 2002, due to an influx
of non-Irish speaking property buyers. The problem is exacerbated
by the fact that the low density of population in many Gaeltacht
areas makes it harder for their inhabitants to practice the language
regularly.[7]

Far from their own countries, immigrants – Poles, English,
Germans and Spanish – can switch effortlessly between their
native language and English. Several Dublin bars provide Ireland's

56,000 officially estimated Polish immigrants with venues to speak Polish.[8] In their own country, most of the 1.7 million Irish speakers have no such opportunity.

REVIVING THE REVIVAL

A century ago, a Celtic cultural revival began, as playwrights, poets and academic scholars began rebuilding and modernising Gaelic culture. As they struggle to revive Irish a century later, language activists can draw inspiration from two sources. Firstly, it has been done before under far more challenging circumstances. Secondly, raising children in two languages promotes a child's later ability in life, particularly at learning languages.

As the first Celtic cultural revival was taking place, another language was making a stunning comeback. Hebrew had died out as a spoken language in the third century after Christ but had, for religious purposes, been preserved in written form.[9] Undaunted by the 1,700 year gap, Hebrew language activists set to work to revive the language in the late nineteenth century. A little over a century later, Hebrew is now spoken by five million Israelis. The man responsible for the revival – Eliezer Ben-Yehuda – would have a few things to say about the Irish educational system's approach to teaching Gaelic. Hebrew was revived in a strategic manner. Before Israel even became independent, schools and homes were targeted as the vital cradle of revival. If children could learn the language at a basic level from a young age, they would have the crucial foundation for fluency later on. If they failed, a huge and possibly unfeasible amount of later learning would be needed to substitute for this.

In more modern times, the policy has been successfully applied to the challenge of a multiracial country with a booming economy. As one of the world's richest economies, Singapore's economic development, and the dramatic influx of people from China and Malaysia, could have upset the delicate linguistic balance between English and Singapore's dialect of Chinese, leading to serious ethnic strife. But with great sophistication, Singapore has understood that language policy needs to carefully balance economic with cultural objectives. To preserve their cultural identity, Chinese, Malay and Tamil languages are taught to children at an early age, an age when a language is easily picked up. As a language of commerce, English is taught for its utilitarian value. In the twentieth century, the English language has lost much of the richness it had in the days of Shakespeare and Edmund Burke; a price it paid for its growing flexibility and widespread usage as a language of commerce. For Ireland, English is not the language that defines us. It is a language we are lucky to have, but only if we have something else: a basic ability to speak our own language.

MIGRATION AND CULTURE

So far, the only such community that exists nationally is a virtual one. As well as recreating a national Irish speaking community, the Irish language television station TG4 is challenging an increasingly sounded but facile assumption about our national culture: that the main threat to it comes from immigration. Of Dutch extraction, Alex Hijmans started to learn Irish when he came to Ireland some years ago. He became so fluent that he is now a regular newsreader on TG4. And yet, despite his example, we are still as a nation pointing the finger at immigrants.

During the summer of 2007 a young and civic-minded Irishman of the Sikh religion volunteered to serve on the Garda Reserve Force. The force was a newly created body that allowed willing citizens to help the full-time Garda force by performing basic community policing tasks. Like Hijmans, here was someone making a contribution to the welfare of the country. But the Garda Commissioner's office refused the man[10] permission to wear a garment essential to the profession of his religion. Caught between his religious beliefs and his desire to help the community, the man was forced to withdraw his services. It was a choice he should not have been forced to make.

Condemning the move, a Sikh policeman in the UK, where the turban is permitted, pointed out that he didn't cease to be a Sikh when he went into work. The minister of state with responsibility for Integration, Conor Lenihan, defended the move saying, 'If we are to take integration seriously, people who come here must understand our way of doing things.'[11] But the question begged asking: integration into what? Here is a nation gradually losing all traces of identity and uniqueness, trying to integrate someone into a culture that will soon cease to exist. On the cusp of the twenty-first century, just what cultural values are we trying to integrate immigrants into?

There are a few bright spots on the cultural horizon. Breaking an assumption maintained in earlier chapters – that the market is always right – TG4 is an example of how, in the initial phases of its incubation or restoration, culture cannot be left to the market. As the physical Gaeltacht fights a rearguard action, the virtual Gaeltacht creates a repository for safe keeping, one that will keep the language alive until – as was done in Israel with Hebrew – vibrant Irish-speaking communities can be recreated.

But apart from TG4, all too often Ireland is trading in its cultural identity for an uncertain future. It is a country where the odd, occasional and superficial nod to Irishness is a cold, rainy day attending a sanitised, sterile Saint Patrick's Day parade; an event from which the Saint himself – like the Sikh and his turban – has been banished as a religious undesirable.

EDUCATION AND CULTURE

The real threat to Irish culture doesn't come from immigrants. In 2005, Alex Hijmans and Australian translator Ariel Killick established iMeasc, a group of fluent Irish speaking immigrants. Half-Fijian brothers Seán Óg and Setanta Ó hAilpín and half-Korean Jason Sherlock are major stars of hurling and Gaelic football. No, the real source of the threat is elsewhere.

By 2006, one in six 'native' Irish school pupils were failing Irish language tests, while the media was reporting a growing sense of disillusionment amongst Irish teachers[12] about the future of the language. And yet, as iMeasc was lobbying for state-funded Irish classes for immigrant children living in Gaeltacht areas or close to Gaelscoileanna, Fine Gael was questioning the role of immigrants in Irish culture. In an important speech on immigration, Fine Gael leader Enda Kenny referred to the Irish as a Celtic people.[13] In a remark that would have been laughable were it no so stupid, Kenny said that in order to integrate, immigrants would have to learn English. More than anything else, the speech encapsulates the confusion and dysfunction at the heart of our attitude to culture and migration.

The failure of the Spatial Strategy is compounding that dysfunction. The Gaeltacht is under relentless attack. English-speaking house buyers are moving into the Gaeltacht to enjoy its high quality of life. At the same time, unwittingly, they are destroying it. Ignoring the motto 'When in Rome do as the Romans do', the newcomers are complaining about the lack of English education in local schools. If economics – a desire to make their offspring fluent in the language of commerce – is one driving factor in their demands, ignorance is another. Like bilingual children in other parts of Europe, children who speak solely Irish at school and English with friends or family are more intelligent and better at languages generally. The more languages one learns, the easier it becomes to learn another. But, like the Fine Gael Party, some parents in the area of An Daingean[14] see their children faced with a straight choice between Irish or English. Instead of blaming the state, parents opposed to teaching through Irish turn their ire against local Irish-speaking families, families who have been there for generations and are merely trying to defend their way of life. As the last areas where Irish is spoken as a native language teeter on the brink of extinction, another example of how the state's failure to plan for population growth is having disastrous results.

At no stage has the Irish government asked why the Danish, Finnish, Dutch, Belgian and Swiss educational systems can raise children with two and sometimes three languages, while Ireland's education system can't get past one. Even though several generations have been let down in this respect as children, the state has not incentivised them to take up the language as adults. There are tax breaks for trade union subscriptions, but not for learning Irish. The government is – rightly – willing to fund TG4. But it is not willing to put the population in a position where it can actually use it. iMeasc is asking the government to help immigrants learn Irish, something too few Irish are doing for themselves.

Ireland has spent the last two centuries dissipating its identity, giving to foreign countries and wars a populace that should have been used for its own growth and prosperity. It is emigration, not immigration, that has devastated Ireland's cultural heritage. Until the seventeenth century, even foreign invaders – Vikings, Normans and English – ended up adopting native customs and culture. With their Fijian, Vietnamese and Dutch origins, Seán Óg Ó hAilpín, Jason Sherlock and Alex Hijmans represent a return to this tradition.

Ireland's revival in the coming century must be cultural as well as economic. Recovering spoken Irish amongst the population – something Israel has shown can be done – and consolidating the physical Gaeltacht are the two main challenges. Unless we turn them into enemies, immigrants are likely allies in these challenges. The language and traditions of Ireland are just as accessible to them – regardless of colour, creed or taste in headgear – as to those born here.

CHAPTER 14

The Curse of Class

An American will look up at somebody living in a big house on a hill and say, 'Someday, I'm going to be like him.' An Irishman will look up at the big house and say, 'Someday, I'm going to get that fecker!'

Bono

A Part of Who We Are

For decades it was blamed for economic failure. But to many people 'begrudgery' isn't a historical illness, rather it is a proud tradition and one with a long pedigree. In the summer of 2006 this tradition was alive and well as the public reaction to a decision by Dublin rock band U2 to move their financial affairs to the Netherlands was to prove. Writer Brendan O'hEithir described the Irish begrudger as having the memory of an elephant and the mind of a grasshopper. As far as U2 were concerned, he was to be proved wrong at least on the first count. As they deplored U2's actions, some commentators were to display the memory of a fly. One of the world's biggest rock bands, U2 had created hundreds, perhaps thousands, of jobs in Ireland. They had paid millions, perhaps tens of millions, in tax revenues to the Irish Exchequer in corporation tax, income and Value Added Tax (VAT). As ambassadors for their country they lifted and modernised the image of Ireland in a way that no government or Bord Fáilte[1] PR agency could conceive of, never mind give effect to.

In the letters, pages and blogs that registered reaction to the move, U2's decision was put in contrast to its lead singer Bono's frequent calls to increase funding for the world's poor. As if there was any comparison. Together with other bands, U2 have raised more money in relief aid than several governments put together. Like many Irish people, they had become tired of paying taxes to a state that spent them, not on the world's or even Ireland's poorest, but on the often questionable whims of the public sector.

Even after they joined the flight of tax earls,[2] U2 continues to generate millions for the Exchequer. It doesn't matter: begrudgery remains a feature of the national psyche. Many have written about it but few have really outlined why it is important. One exception, Cathal Guiomard,[3] concluded that it was a social disease. But what if it was something else, a symptom rather than a cause of a deeper social problem?

THE CURSE OF CLASS

When the 2004 local elections resulted in a strong vote for Sinn Féin, not everyone was surprised. Combining a blend of left-wing economics and nationalist politics that was almost unique in the EU, the party caught a wave of deep disaffection that was sweeping over the country. It was a decade since the ESRI had first predicted the boom in its medium-term forecast of spring 1994.

In an era of full employment – and with a basic minimum wage in operation – it is becoming harder for the Left to make its case. But it tries hard. Despite growing average incomes – particularly amongst the lowest paid – and the introduction of a minimum wage, the perception is rife that Ireland is an 'unfair' society. The Left denounces the lack of public spending, even though public expenditure has increased dramatically since 1997. Setting out a social democratic vision, the left-wing group tasc argue that the state needs to increase government spending as a share of GDP. Like most of the Left in Ireland – including some in Fianna Fáil – it sees the state as a magic box that can turn extra spending into all kinds of good things.

The results are totally to the contrary. In 2002, UCD professor and leading accountant Niamh Brennan chaired a study into the performance of the health sector, one of the largest areas of state spending. Despite massive increases in health spending between 1997 and 2002 – in both absolute and proportionate terms – performance metrics in the sector such as in-patient treatment and patient discharges had increased in paltry single-digit figures. The problem with state spending isn't its extent, but its design and the lack of reform accompanying it.

Nonetheless, sensing a changing wind, Taoiseach Bertie Ahern proclaimed himself a 'socialist' in September of 2004 and invited anti-poverty activist Father Seán Healy to address the Fianna Fáil parliamentary party think-in. A year later, Robert Putnam, US sociologist and author of *Bowling Alone*[4] was invited. On both occasions there was much talk of the promise in the 1916 Proclamation to 'cherish the children of the nation equally'. The idea was to reconnect with the public and empathise with the less well-off. But if Ireland's recent past proves anything, it is that the state's attempts to cherish anything have come to nothing. Cherishing is a task best left to family and friends and doesn't need the input of politicians. But as the state wastes its time cherishing us, our relationships with family and friends are suffering as the state fails to do what it should be doing: ensuring proper spatial and urban planning, good transport and competitive markets. By empathising with our feelings, politicians are distracting us and themselves from their own failure.

As the Left makes inroads into the establishment, right-wing opinion is stirring in response. In a contribution that would have been unthinkable some years before, Progressive Democrat TD and Minister for Justice Michael McDowell defended the existence of inequality as a necessary incentive. As well as perceived losers, the boom had created real winners, winners who had made their own way without state support and who didn't feel the need to pay any more tax to the state.

Politically, Ahern and McDowell were more similar than they made out. Socially, they could not have been more different. Proud of his roots, Ahern is a working-class Dubliner with an affinity to the trade union movement. Economically pragmatic, he is also capable of populism when the need arises. As Attorney General in the 1997–2002 government and Minister for Justice between 2002 and 2007, McDowell was part of a government that brought in a minimum wage and increases in state spending that any socialist in Europe would have been proud of. And yet, for many, he represented something that undermined the truth of what he was saying: the role of privilege in determining economic status.

Since its foundation, Ireland has shifted its class structure. It may be warping the economy but, as a determinant of social status, the ownership of land and property counts for very little these days. Mercifully, it has been replaced by something more meritocratic – the ability to secure wages and a salary in a competitive and dynamic labour market.[5] The problem with this brave new world, however, is that access to education remains largely determined by social background. Sociologists Breen and Whelan noted in the early years of the Celtic Tiger, 'despite increasing overall levels of educational attainment the pattern of educational social fluidity has remained unaltered. There is a continuing strong link between class origins and educational attainment.'[6] A great race for prosperity began in the mid-1990s. It was unfortunately a race in which different competitors had very different starting points.

The link was spatial as well as class-oriented. A triangle of privilege in the Dublin area is defined by Terenure and Rathgar in the west and Howth and Killiney in the east, a triangle perpetuated as much by a local mentality – one that fosters aspiration and encouragement – as by access to better schools. As of 2007, Sutton Park School in Howth is charging boarder students over €22,000 a year to enjoy a heated outdoor pool and astroturf sports pitches. Within three miles of this school, in Dublin's north inner city, schools are struggling to provide basic educational facilities. One study found that, in inner-city Dublin, the reading ability of over a third of children, 35 per cent, is several years behind the national average. In wealthy Rathgar, no children suffer this disability.

McDowell was and remains correct: imposing income equality on people of unequal abilities is futile. But he was also incomplete.

In justifying his own astounding achievements, McDowell could point to a career based on hard work and merit. But others could point to something else: the privilege of an education that very few in the state have access to. And more besides: a vocabulary, a social-isation, a lexicon of ambition and achievement, that, regardless of his formal education, would set the expectations for him and his kind far higher than other citizens of the state.

Is begrudgery towards success really unjustified? Or is it that inequality in Ireland is intolerable not because it exists, but because of where it comes from. McDowell challenged the compassion bab-ble of equality and, fundamentally, he was right. From the evil of totalitarianism to the dull mediocrity of social democracy, this is a doctrine that has failed mankind in whatever form it has been tried. When not accompanied by absolute poverty, inequality is a crucial incentive to achievement. But if meritocracy is to work and also be socially acceptable, it needs one other caveat: the existence of equal opportunity.

His self-proclaimed socialism aside, Ahern epitomises meritoc-racy. Devoid of wealthy parents or an especially good education, Ahern rose to the top on merit. He continues to preside over one of the most successful free enterprise economies in the world. Here is someone with the credibility to fight for equal opportunity in edu-cation. Yet he has spent much of his years in office defending inde-fensibly backward practices in the public sector. The right messenger is carrying the wrong message; the messenger with the right one doesn't know how to deliver it.

POVERTY AND SPACE

The Combat Poverty Agency has reported that, as late as 2007, some 290,000 people continue to live in poverty.[7] Based as it is on a broad definition, the figure may be somewhat overstated. Poverty is a multi-dimensional concept with many different methodologies to measure it. But exist in Ireland it does and, as an earlier report by Combat Poverty makes crystal clear, its spatial dimension is unavoidable.[8] The report, which examines patterns of poverty at regional and county level, shows conclusively that the risk of poverty and unemployment is highest in the remotest parts of the state, especially in Donegal, Leitrim and Mayo. Poverty is lowest in Dublin, by far the most urbanised part of the state. The number of elderly living alone is highest in north Connacht and the border county areas, where want of opportunity has caused those who otherwise might have looked after their parents to leave. As well as warping the productivity of regional economies, the state's failure to reap the density dividend has also left its mark on the country's poor.

MEANWHILE, BACK AT THE KIBBUTZ

On top of spatial dysfunction, Ireland suffers from social dysfunction, the legacy of a British class system that it never fully shook off after independence. Also once ruled by Britain, Israel has been far more successful in this regard. A state where seven million people from radically different economic and cultural backgrounds were thrown together relatively suddenly might have produced a cauldron of social division and conflict. But, relative to the part of the world in which it is located, the social cohesion between Israel's immigrant and native born citizens is – whatever about the lack of cohesion between Arabs and Jews – remarkable. The army was one reason for this cohesion. More than just a means of defence, for the many new Israelis passing through its ranks, it was a crucial agent of naturalisation and socialisation – creating common bonds of association between people as different as chalk and cheese.

Another crucial institution in Israel was the kibbutz. In many countries capitalism had achieved an inequality that was too influenced by the inheritance of wealth, accent or privileged experience. The kibbutzim tried to strike a balance, creating communities based on voluntary collectivism. At its strongest in the 1930s, the kibbutz movement created solidarity amongst enough of Israel's first immigrants to see the state through its most intensive phase of growth. Could a similar institution play a role in Ireland?

CHAPTER 15

1607–2007: The Return of the Earls

Migration increases the urgency of existing policy challenges more than it creates entirely new ones.

Government report on Migration Policy, 2006

BACK TO THE FUTURE (AGAIN)

After two amazing decades of transformation, Ireland remains half the nation that it could be. Its population density is amongst the lowest in the developed world. For this reason, Ireland is rich in a resource that the world is running out of: land that is not just habitable but that is located in a part of the world where prosperity, the rule of law and free and fair government are strong. As it draws capital, technology and people from overpopulated and underdevelopment countries around it, Ireland is recovering from a stunted past with rapid speed. Forecasts of nine million people by the year 2050 in the Republic, and twelve million on the island, are high but conceivable. The problem is that Ireland's ability to defend its culture and identity – a culture and identity nearly destroyed by overseas migration – will depend on the source of that growth. The first source is continued immigration from the world's developing or partly developed countries. The second is a return of the Diaspora. The third is the recovery of Ireland's fertility levels to above population replacement levels. So far, there is much of the first and only a trickle of the second. And as far as natural population increase is concerned, the outlook is worrying: Ireland is failing to replace its population naturally, that is through childbirth rather than immigration.

From negligible levels a generation ago, the share of those living in the Republic of Ireland but born outside it now stands at more than one in ten of the population. The share of workers born outside the state has now reached one in nine.[1] Between 2002 and 2006, the state's population increased by 319,000 people, by almost one-tenth. One-third of these were Eastern Europeans who came here to work.

Some 'Irish' remigration has indeed occurred. Born in Ireland and having spent too little time abroad to sever personal and cultural links with their home country, boomerang migrants returned in their tens of thousands during the 1990s. But this is not the Diaspora. For them – most of whom live in the US or UK – today's Ireland is too expensive and not different enough from their present Anglo-Saxon environment. By 2006, barely 5 per cent of immigrants were from the US or UK. According to the 2006 Census, only 18,174 of the non-Irish working in Ireland are of Irish descent. There are more Lithuanians than that and almost three times as many Poles.

Had the Diaspora made up a significant chunk of the one-third of a million who came here between 2002 and 2006, Ireland's recent migration story might be very different. In the film *The Field*, Bull McCabe confronts an Irish emigrant returning from America who is trying to buy a field McCabe himself has been saving for decades to buy himself. 'Ye went off to America. But we stayed. We stayed!' McCabe screams, before eventually killing him. Wealthier than the Poles, and more ambitious, the Diaspora would not be content with the low wage jobs that most recent immigrants have taken. Research has shown that immigrants from accession states are on average earning 30 per cent less than their Irish-born counterparts, and that this differential is accounted for mainly by well-qualified immigrants performing low skilled work.[2] By contrast, the Diaspora would expect high income and high status jobs, not to mention houses in desirable parts of the country. How this competition for jobs and property would be regarded is an open question.

In some ways, the success of immigration to date partly reflects its non-Irish character. Immigrants from non-Irish backgrounds are not wealthy, more hungry for opportunity and therefore more willing to fit into the cultural situation that greets them. Most of all, they are generally free of that habit most irritating to the rooted Irish: the annoying desire to improve the country.

On a more optimistic note, if Ireland's spatial dysfunction and high house prices are dealt with systematically and over time, this could become a place to where some of the Diaspora would want to return. The third and higher generation Irish are largely a lost cause: their roots in their host country are too deep and the compensating advantages of returning to Ireland are too low. For the first and second generation Irish – numbering anything between one and three million – the story is a different one. But for two important reasons, population growth from this source will have to be complemented by an increase from the other two sources.

Relying entirely on immigration for population growth – from the Diaspora or otherwise – is unhealthy and politically dangerous. The nation's cultural future should depend on those born and raised here. Ireland's poor population performance up until the 1990s stemmed not just from emigration, but, as a historically high marriage age testifies, also from the inability of the economy to provide potential young couples with the incomes they needed to raise families. Now that the incomes are finally available to them, the cost of living, especially of accommodation in commutable areas, has risen, recreating an old problem under a new guise. Urban sprawl, high house prices and long commutes have caused many couples to delay marriage and family formation beyond the EU norm. A fundamental redesign of our towns and cities isn't just a good idea from an economic productivity point of view. Together with improving childcare facilities, it is also consistent with enabling women to balance work with child rearing, again something the state needs to do, regardless of the pressures of population growth.

If a degree of natural population increase is important for cultural reasons, immigration from outside the Diaspora will be important for economic ones. Constantin Gurdgiev notes how migration from Eastern Europe acts as a thermostat in Ireland's high price economy, preventing wage pressures from overheating too much, a benefit the Diaspora could never give.[3] As the advantage of this diminishes over time, a new imperative in immigration policy arises: the need to attract high quality workers not just from fellow EU member states but from any country in the world that has them. Again, our spatial dysfunction and high cost economy is a barrier. Of the tens of thousands of Irish who emigrated to the US in living memory, many are highly skilled and would return if the cost and quality of living could, respectively, be lowered and raised. Along with the Irish born are the second generation Irish whose folk memories may be strong enough to entice them. But, according to Gurdgiev, Ireland's approach to migration cuts the economy off from a vital supply of low cost skills sets we will badly need in the future. As the government's strategy shifts towards encouraging the traded service sector, immigration policy needs to be redesigned accordingly.

The question of who we let in goes hand-in-hand with that of where we put them when they come here. The low wage status of immigrants is increasingly reflected in their spatial distribution. Forty-four per cent of the population living between Parnell Street and Dorset Street was born outside of Ireland. As Limerick City's population fell by 2.7 per cent between 2002 and 2006, its non-national population rose by 42.5 per cent. As happened in US city centres thirty years ago, the affluent natives are moving out as the low paid migrants move in. One-quarter of the population of Loughlinstown and Springfield – two populous Dublin suburbs – are non-national. One area, Blanchardstown, saw its non-national population rise by 120 per cent between 2002 and 2006.

During economic downturns, the low income sectors of the economy get hit hardest. The cheek by jowl concentration of immigrants in some areas of the country – currently a symptom of a property boom and the high house prices that go with it – could become a symptom of social and cultural division as that boom subsides and low income jobs disappear.

In the 1970s and 1980s, Israel's social cohesion began to feel the strains of rapid growth. Class struggle began to re-emerge. In 1988, President Herzog warned, 'We are witness to violence in industrial relations, and the conduct of industrial struggle on the back of the ordinary citizen.'[4] Ireland is preparing to assimilate hundreds of thousands if not millions more people into the country, people of differing backgrounds who will some day find themselves jostling for jobs and position. It is also still dealing with chronic inequality of opportunity amongst its native born citizens. How can we make sure Herzog's words don't some day apply to Ireland?

Social strife is usually sparked by economic difference, but it needs a further ingredient: a cultural difference that creates a perception of unfairness. That unfairness is either discrimination – the native getting a job that the immigrant deserves – or a failure to discriminate – the immigrant taking what the native feels is his. The solution to this advocated by some – that Ireland should adapt and change its culture to suit immigrants – will only exacerbate any future conflict. A country whose economy is under pressure will suffer more conflict if it feels its identity is being threatened too. The best way to fortify Ireland against the strains and stresses of immigration is to do exactly the reverse: to strengthen its traditions and identity.

This doesn't require discriminating in favour of immigration from the Diaspora. Although mostly Jewish, Israel's immigrants were often radically different from each other in almost all other respects, having grown apart in different cultures for centuries. Nonetheless, Israel has preserved a common culture. Moreover, it has resurrected a language that had been dead in spoken form for over a millennium and a half. The situation in Ireland is almost the reverse. Despite immigration, Ireland is still largely a mono-racial country, since immigrants and native Irish have not yet intermarried to any significant degree. But Ireland is losing its language and culture, becoming little different from any Anglo-Saxon country. Far from threatening those traditions, most immigrants are blank sheets of paper, willing recipients of the culture they emigrate to. If they seem to cling to their own culture, maybe it is because Ireland has nothing better to offer. Our education system is failing to preserve the Irish language. With few exceptions, the mass media is drawing us towards a culturally uncertain future.

Forging a common culture between immigrants and the Irish born – one that preserves the best of Ireland's past but is flexible enough to be adopted by newcomers – is the answer. If we can look to Israel for demographic inspiration, we can also do so for cultural inspiration. In 1930s, 1940s and 1950s, the kibbutz was a source of common identity that defined for newcomers who they were. Together with military conscription, the kibbutz did something else; something Ireland needs to do today. Israelis who had trained for combat together were far less likely to uphold a class system, with all the resentments, begrudgery and social dysfunction that comes with it. Never mind any future conflict between the Irish born and immigrants, the fall in support for the state's main political parties during the 2004 local elections was a piquant whiff of what can happen when a significant part of the electorate feels economically marginalised. But this was in a time of prosperity. Tougher economic times could cause conflict between Irish-born workers and immigrant workers with lower expectations of pay and conditions.

On top of ethnic tensions – and interacting with them – could come social ones. Rising wealth in Ireland has not been equally matched by rising equality of opportunity. The rise of grind schools and private education has made educational access arguably less equal than before. The Irish state makes no effort whatsoever to build a cohesive citizenry under the age of eighteen, people who can respect each other and accept their respective economic statuses as products of effort rather than privilege. Although only 2 per cent of Israel's population now lives in kibbutzim permanently, this does not represent their importance in citizen building. Many more temporary visitors have experienced a sharing of culture and values. Although imperfect and not as cohesive as before, Israel does not suffer the magnitude of Ireland's class system. In Ireland, the nearest thing to spending time in the kibbutzim is going to the Gaeltacht.

From being the home of spoken Irish and language schools, could the Gaeltacht become something more important?

Short of nationalising or radically harmonising the secondary educational experience – or introducing military conscription – Ireland has no mechanism to create a common cultural and economic socialisation of its young. Neither has it – unlike the US – worked out a systematic approach to naturalising its new citizens. If a Republic means anything, it means forging a common citizenship. And if Irishness means anything, it means culture. There is little appetite in Ireland for military conscription. But generations of secondary students have gone to the Gaeltacht for the summer.

Citizen building and cultural development are as important a part of education as science or maths. And some way will have to be found to naturalise the many hundreds of thousands of adults likely to come here in the coming decades. The summer schools of the Gaeltacht are – together with the various summer schools in which major issues of the day are hammered out, such as the Merriman Schools – are drawing boards on which finding a solution to this problem should commence. If formalised, they could become something new: a way of inculcating Irish culture and identity in the young but also – in a different format – a way of moulding new citizens from abroad.

As well as citizens, any state needs an aristocracy; not a hereditary one based on privilege but one based on the republican values of equal opportunity and advancement by hard work and merit. Like its peasants and artisans, Ireland has lost its fair share of these in the past. As this book was in the final stages of writing,[5] Ireland – North and South – is commemorating the four hundredth anniversary of the Flight of the Earls. In 1607, the self-exiled Hugh O'Neill languished in Rome, cut off from his homeland.

Four hundred years later, much of the new Irish aristocracy still finds itself abroad, but these days it laughs at distance. In London, Peter Sutherland is chairman of British Petroleum and also UN Commissioner for Migration. In the latter role he follows in the footsteps of former UN Human Rights Commissioner Mary Robinson who, as president of Ireland, was the first head of state to fully recognise the global nature of the Irish nation. Willie Walsh runs British Airways, while Michael O'Leary is redefining the airline industry across the EU. Denis O'Brien runs a global telecommunications empire stretching from the Caribbean to the Atlantic, and Anthony O'Reilly owns a media empire stretching from the UK to South Africa. But all of these people remain participants in the economic, social and cultural life of their homeland. Ireland's reputation for creating world leaders goes beyond the world of business. Bertie Ahern's achievement in steering EU heads of government to agree to an EU constitution in 2003 remains – in spite of its subsequent defeat – an achievement of historical and international stature. In 2007, the main session of the World Economic Forum in Davos was chaired by Bono. The central podium of the session assembled to discuss world poverty was made up of ten global leaders including then UK Prime Minister Tony Blair. Three of them, including Bono, were Irish.

Whether in business, politics, music or cinema, Ireland is contributing to the world out of all proportion to the size of the Irish state. And that, as sure as anything, is a sign that the present Irish state is too small. At just 4.2 million souls in the Republic and 6 million on the island, Ireland's present size cannot begin to do justice to the huge potential of the Irish. Four hundred years after leaving, the earls are coming home; a great circle of history is closing. Many more – of Irish and non-Irish extraction – are following. If we can build a country fit for them, then the best is yet to come. If we will it, it is no dream.

1707–2007: Scotland's Choice

Despite being twin nations – with comparable histories, similar sized populations and very similar cultures – Ireland and Scotland couldn't be in more different positions relative to each other than they are today. Both countries have had to struggle to build economies on the edge of the European continent and in the shadow of a large neighbour. With its emphasis on having a central location close to markets, the laws of economic development have not been kind to either nation. In the nineteenth century, however, Scotland made remarkable strides in industry, commerce and finance. The cultural price paid has left deep economic and cultural marks. Once flourishing centres of population, Scotland's highland areas gave way to an industrial belt running between Glasgow and Edinburgh, an economic powerhouse that declined as the twentieth century went on. The exploitation of oil reserves since the 1970s has provided a strong counterweight to more recent claims that today's Scotland lives off transfers from Westminster.

That is, sadly, not the greatest of Scotland's problems. Some sources estimate that Scotland's population will fall by a quarter of a million over the course of the next generation.[1] In the last decade, the population of the island of Ireland overtook that of Scotland. By 2019, the population of the twenty-six counties of the Republic of Ireland will be greater than that of Scotland. Scotland has the lowest life expectancy in the OECD. If demographic recovery is to go hand-in-hand with prosperity, a resurgence in Scotland's population needs to be complemented by something more: greater autonomy in economic policy. Scotland also faces the strong gravitational pull of England's economy, which is creating the kind of brain drain that paralysed the Republic of Ireland in the first six decades of the state's existence.

At five million, Scotland's population is, like Ireland's, relatively low by the standards of the other non-Nordic countries of Western Europe (most of Scotland's climate is temperate). A figure of eight million by the end of the century would not be outrageous, were there economic conditions to support it. Like Ireland, Scotland has a relatively smaller but still significant Diaspora, many of whom live in England.

In what appears to be a vicious circle, Scotland is underperforming its peers. GDP growth in Ireland averaged 5.2 per cent in the twenty-five years leading up to and including 2005. In Norway, where population growth was more stable and demographic change more mild, the average was 3.1 per cent. In Scotland, GDP growth in this period was just 1.8 per cent. As of 2007, just as Gordon Brown, a Scot, became Prime Minister of the UK, Scotland's contribution to the UK Exchequer was declining. While in Ireland they were falling for the good reason that they had grown too fast, land and property price falls in Scotland are more deeply rooted in demographic and economic trends. Like Ireland in the 1950s and other regions of Britain today, Scotland's brightest and best are fleeing south.

According to a leading competitiveness yearbook, Scotland ranks thirtieth globally in competitiveness terms, well behind Ireland, Denmark, Norway and Finland and far below Scotland's potential. A nation that invented the television, the telephone, Penicillin, not to mention economics, Scotland is a country without whose genius the modern world would be unthinkable. Apart from native genius, Scotland was the location – but not the beneficiary – of massive oil reserves that, had they been in the hands of an independent Scotland, would have allowed Scotland to overcome the legacy of Union.

That legacy was not without its positive aspects. From the mid-nineteenth to the mid-twentieth century, Scotland benefited from the demands of a growing British Empire for its heavy industrial produce. As Ireland sank into decline, Scotland flourished. By the 1970s, the emergence of low-cost Asian economies ended Scotland's comparative advantage, pushing up unemployment. Oil revenues might have played the same role in helping Scotland to adapt to this new environment that EU funding did in kick starting Ireland's domestic economy.

As the south of England prospered, Scotland's economy continued to deteriorate up until the early 1990s. Had Union not prevented it, a lower tax regime for Scotland might have rebalanced the relative attractiveness of Scotland relative to England. Again had the Union not prevented it, a commitment to joining the euro might have created an attractive base for multinationals to locate. Unlike most of Ireland, there has always been a strong support for the Union in Scotland. Far from being invaded, Scotland voluntarily merged its monarchy with that of England. In 1707, like its Irish counterpart almost a hundred years later, the Scottish parliament voted to merge with that of England and Wales. Like in the Irish case, the decision was not uninfluenced by bribery. Three hundred years have not extinguished the cause of independence, however. Exactly three hundred years later and for the first time ever opinion polls north and south of Hadrian's Wall show a majority of Scots and English favouring Scottish independence. They also show the Scottish National Party, led by economist Alex Salmond MP, enjoying a consistent lead over other parties in Scotland. Next May – three hundred years after joining the Union – Scots may decide to begin managing their own economy.

Until recently, the idea of Scottish independence would have been seen as a far-fetched response to Scotland's problems. In 2006, former Royal Bank of Scotland chief and leading British banker George Mathewson endorsed the concept. Even in England – a country increasingly more concerned with defining its own identity rather than that of its neighbours – recent opinion polls show a majority of English voters supporting the idea. Little wonder this, since the English taxpayer subsidises Scotland to a significant degree.

Scottish migration to London is also a significant contribution to the chronic spatial imbalance in the UK as a whole, over one-third of whose inhabitants now live in south-east England. Serious constitutional and political issues are at stake. But whatever about the constitutional issues, the case for Scottish economic independence seems unarguable. Geographic peripherality can still hinder an economy that is underperforming, especially one with a falling population. The ability to achieve and maintain a lower tax burden compared to England could be vital in reviving Scotland's fortunes.

In 2006, the then UK Chancellor Gordon Brown lowered the UK's rate of corporation tax from 30 to 28 per cent. But with a host of competitor nations, including Ireland and the accession states of Eastern Europe, having rates of between 12 and 20 per cent, Scotland's rate needs to be lower, much lower. Despite being traditionally to the left of Labour, the Scottish National Party has strongly embraced the doctrine of cutting corporation and income taxes. No UK Prime Minister – particularly not a Scot like Brown – can advocate a lower tax regime for the country he comes from while asking his English voters to pay higher taxes. For that reason independence is the only way to achieve the leverage that Scotland needs to correct its present predicament. Tax independence is also important from another point of view: tax revenues from oil reserves off Scotland's coast are no longer what they were. But the power to divert such taxes as are paid from London to Edinburgh would be crucial in compensating for a subsidy from London that – in the event of independence – would in the long-term be politically unacceptable from an English point of view.

The issue of monetary independence is also important. Scottish parliamentarians have retained the ability to print banknotes, in spite of the Union. Euro membership – possible under independence – would nonetheless put Scotland in a difficult position. Its trade is with England. But then again membership of a four hundred million strong currency union is likely to put Scotland in a much more attractive position than it is at present when seeking to attract foreign direct investment. Together with Scotland's low cost of living, the benefits of lower taxes, oil revenues and membership of the euro – could provide a powerful impetus to economic and demographic recovery, without breaking Scotland's link with the Crown. Fiscal and monetary autonomy would not have to come at the expense of preserving links with England. A united monarchy would still unite Scotland with England and Wales. Neither would independence incur any penalties. By virtue of EU membership, Scotland's access to England's markets for goods and services and the free movement of its people within the EU would be secure.

Until very recently, Scottish independence was considered unthinkable. But, in 2007, the unthinkable happened. Exactly three hundred years after that independence ended and just across the water from Scotland's western coast, Ian Paisley and Gerry Adams agreed to share power in a devolved Northern Ireland government. On the whole island, decades of mistrust and hostility are being replaced by cooperation as an increasingly united economy emerges. For Scotland as well as Ireland, the unthinkable is becoming more and more thinkable.

Notes

INTRODUCTION

1. Coleman, M., 'State is Ill-prepared for Future Population Growth,' *Irish Times*, 31 March 2006.

CHAPTER 1 – BACK TO THE FUTURE

1. United Nations Population Time Series.
2. Figures supplied by the Embassy of Israel to Ireland.
3. Author's own interpolation from the 1851 and 1861 Censuses.
4. Author's own calculation based on latest UK census data (2001) and the land masses of Ireland and England.
5. United Nations, *World Population Prospects: The 2006 Revision*.
6. The different years of comparison for Ireland (2006) and other countries affects the comparison between Ireland's current population and potential population as defined by other countries, but not to a significant degree for the point being illustrated.
7. Gallup, J.L., Sachs, J.D. and Mellinger, A.D., *Geography and Economic Development*, NBER Working Paper 6849, December 1998.
8. Like Malthus' predictions in the nineteenth century that rapid population growth would lead to famine, this finding may weaken over time as medicine and technology – everything from malaria vaccines to air conditioning – render economic growth more immune to regional climates.
9. United Nations, *World Population Prospects: The 2006 Revision*.
10. Depending on fertility trends, it could be somewhere between 7.8 billion and 10.8 billion.

11. Published in March 2006. The authors were Eunan King and Dermot O'Brien.
12. Mary Robinson, 3 December 1990, as cited in Akenson, D.H., *The Irish Diaspora: A Primer*, 1993.
13. Stripping out the upward impact on the value of production caused by inflation.
14. GDP growth in volume terms was 5.6 per cent, while the labour force grew by 4.6 per cent. Department of Finance, *Budgetary and Economic Statistics 2007*.
15. National Economic and Social Council, *Migration Policy*, September 2006.

CHAPTER 2 – STUNTED NATION

1. Mulqueen, E., report in the *Irish Times*, August 2007.
2. Haughton, J. in O'Hagan, J., *The Economy of Ireland*, 2004.
3. Foster, R.F., *Modern Ireland*, 1972.
4. Northern Ireland Statistics and Research Agency, 2002 Census.
5. Ó Gráda, C. and O'Rourke, K., 'Mass Migration as Disaster Relief', in Ó Gráda, C., *Ireland's Great Famine*, 2006.
6. Limited deaths occurred in those countries as a result.
7. Introduced in 1690, in the wake of the succession of King William III, the Penal Laws also prevented Catholics from voting, taking public office, and entering professional life.
8. Haughton, J. in O'Hagan, J., *The Economy of Ireland*, 2004.
9. According to the UK 2001 Census, Yorkshire and the Humber region – regional areas corresponding to Yorkshire's traditional boundaries – had a population of 4.9 million.
10. Hatton, T. and Williamson, J., *The Age of Mass Migration*, 1998.
11. Mankiw, G., Romer, D. and Weil, D., *A Contribution to the Empirics of Economic Growth*, 1996.
12. Haughton, J. in O'Hagan, J., *The Economy of Ireland*, 2004.
13. Haughton, J. in O'Hagan, J., *The Economy of Ireland*, 2004.
14. Ó Gráda, C., 'Was the Great Famine just like Modern Famines?' in Poirteir, C., *The Great Irish Famine*, 1995.

15. See, for instance, Knack, S. and Keefer, P., 'Why Don't Poor Countries Catch Up?' in *Economic Inquiry*, Volume 35, 1999.
16. The Act of Union united Ireland and Britain under a single parliament, which sat in London.
17. The Whig movement's philosophical opposition to Irish Catholicism – best expressed by John Wilke's accusation that Edmund Burke 'stank of whisky and potatoes' – lasted until the late nineteenth century. In the seventeenth century, Whigs were nostalgic admirers of Cromwell and generally supportive of the Penal Laws. Later in the nineteenth century, the Whig Party evolved into the Liberal Party and, under Gladstone, became a strong supporter of land reform and Home Rule.
18. 'Laissez' is French for 'to allow' and 'faire' for 'to do'. *Laissez-faire* refers to government policy widespread in the nineteenth century, whereby the government had minimal involvement in the state's economy and in the welfare of the people.
19. O'Cathaoir, B., *The Famine Diary*, 1999.
20. O'Cathaoir, B., *The Famine Diary*, 1999.
21. O'Cathaoir, B., *The Famine Diary*, 1999.
22. Satirical pamphlet, published in 1729, in which Jonathan Swift recommends that the Irish eat their own children as a resolution to economic problems and poverty.
23. In terms of Gross Domestic Product.
24. Baldwin, R. and Wyplosz, C., *The Economics of European Integration*, 2004.
25. Then known as West Germany and excluding the present five states of Thuringia, Saxony-Anhalt, Mecklenburg-Vorpommern, Brandenburg, Saxony and East Berlin (then known as East Germany).
26. This differs from GDP in two respects. It excludes from its calculation of economic output the output of foreign-owned entities operating in Ireland, but includes the output of Irish-owned entities operating abroad. GNP is usually between 10 and 20 per cent lower than GDP.
27. Interview with T.K. Whitaker, May 2006.

CHAPTER 3 – THE DENSITY DIVIDEND

1. Department of Environment, Housing Statistics Bulletin, 2006.
2. Central Statistics Office, 2006 Census of Population, Volume 6: Housing.
3. $216,000 \times 2.8 = 604,800$.
4. The measure used for the study was Gross Domestic Product per person employed.
5. While willing to forecast population until 2050, they were only prepared to forecast economic outcomes until 2020.
6. See Chapter 1.
7. ESRI, *Ex Ante Evaluation of the Investment Priorities for the National Development Plan 2007–2013*, 2006.
8. Central Statistics Office, 2006 Census of Population.
9. At a conservative estimate, these include the census districts of South Dublin, Fingal and Dún Laoghaire-Rathdown.
10. Martin P. and Ottaviano, G.I.P, *Growth and Agglomeration* in International Macroeconomics and International Trade programme areas, Centre for Economic Policy Research (CEPR), Discussion Paper Series No. 1529, November 1996.
11. O'Riain, S., *The Politics of High Tech Growth: Developmental Network States in the Global Economy*, 2004.
12. Audretsch, David B., *Agglomeration and the Location of Innovative Activity* in International Organisation and International Trade programme areas, Centre for Economic Policy Research (CEPR), Discussion Paper Series No. 1974, 1998.
13. Siggins, L., report in the *Irish Times*, 31 August 2002.
14. Büttner, T., Schwager, R. and Stegarescu, D., *Agglomeration, Population Size and the Cost of Providing Public Services*, 2004, as quoted in Morgenroth, E., 'The National Spatial Strategy: Regional, Urban and Rural Development' in the ESRI's evaluation of the 2007–2013 National Development Plan, 2006.
15. Permanent tsb/ESRI House Price Index, July 2007.
16. Guiomard, C., *The Irish Disease*, 1995. Cathal Guiomard is now director general of the Irish Aviation Authority.

17. See Chapter 6.
18. It has rapidly responded to increased demand for houses, pushing up the rate of house building to 85,000 units per year by 2006, an observation not rendered invalid by the doubts cast over whether that increased demand was excessive. As it became apparent that it was, the industry is, as of 2007, rapidly scaling back activity.
19. When measured in the National Accounts by the Central Statistics Office.
20. In May 2007.

CHAPTER 4 – RED BRICKS, BLACK POTATOES

1. Oliver, E., report in the *Irish Times*, 7 November 2005.
2. There are anecdotal stories that even higher multiples were achieved.
3. Central Bank of Ireland, Monthly Credit Statistics, August 2006.
4. Incomes would have risen by around 5 per cent, offsetting some of the overvaluation.
5. Bank of Ireland Asset Management's report on Ireland's wealth, September 2007.
6. This is in terms of private sector debt – the debt of households and non-bank corporations – as a share of Gross Domestic Product. In terms of public sector debt as a share of GDP, Ireland ranks second lowest in the EU, after Luxembourg.
7. As of February 2007.
8. Derived from Central Statistics Office, Q4 National Accounts, 2006.
9. O'Rourke, K., 'Non-Traded and Services Sectors,' in O'Hagan, J., *The Economy of Ireland*, 1991.
10. Author's own calculations based on Department of Finance Exchequer Returns, 2007.
11. Chief economist with National Irish Bank. Citation is from the NIB Quarterly Economic Report, October 2007.
12. The main refinancing facility.
13. Coleman, M., report in the *Irish Times*, 14 June 2007.
14. ESRI Quarterly Economic Commentary, September 2007.

CHAPTER 5 – BRIBES FOR TRIBES

1. Fianna Fáil, meaning 'Soldiers of Destiny', is the largest political party in the state and is centrist in orientation.
2. The delays in deciding and disbursing expenditure programmes mean that, in order for their effects to be noticed by voters before election day, the spending needs to be incurred the year before.
3. An Foras Forbartha, *Regional Development in Ireland*, 1968.
4. de Buitleir, D. and McArdle, P., 'A Look to the Future with an Eye on the Past', paper presented at Dublin Economics Workshop Conference, October 2003. A synopsis of the point is that, comparing Ireland's share of government spending with that of other EU countries is the wrong way of assessing how efficient it is. Although apparently lower, this is because Ireland's dependency ratio – the share of children and pensioners in the population – is very low by EU standards. As well as the lower implied cost of pensions and age-related health care, Ireland spends much less on debt service and defence than other countries. Once these factors are accounted for, Ireland's burden of spending and tax is close to the EU average which, itself, is significantly high compared to emerging economies.
5. At under 20,000 square kilometres, Leinster's land mass is just under 30 per cent of the Republic's total.
6. The Census noted some tendency for population to reduce inside the boundaries of the city proper, as young house buyers fled the high prices of suburbs close to the city centre for commuter towns. But this does not alter the conclusion made above in respect of the growth of the economic area of Dublin, an area now conservatively defined by Dublin County. At 251,241, the price of an average house in Dublin in June 2002 – as recorded by the Permanent tsb/ESRI House Price Index for that month – was 49 per cent higher than the equivalent price outside Dublin.
7. The figures related to 2003 when the data was collected.
8. Author's own calculation, applying 2002 Census population weights to separate 2003 indices for disposable income per person. Source: Central

Statistics Office, 2002 Census of Population; Central Statistics Office, County Incomes and Regional GDP, 2007.

9. IMPACT, *Why Decentralisation isn't Working – the Cost and Service Implications of Decentralisation*, May 2006.
10. IMPACT, *Why Decentralisation isn't Working – the Cost and Service Implications of Decentralisation*, May 2006.
11. The scandal involved the improper appropriation from nursing home residents of the costs of their care.
12. Public Service Benchmarking Body, *Report of the Public Service Benchmarking Body*, June 2002.
13. Irish National Teachers Organisation.
14. Byrne, A., report in the *Irish Times*, April 26 2000.
15. Jim O'Leary, former economist with Davy Stockbrokers.
16. Central Statistics Office, 2006 Census of Population, Volume 6: Housing. Enterprise broadband take-up was higher at 48 per cent as of 2005, according to the National Development Plan 2007–2013.

CHAPTER 6 – CAIN SLEW ABEL

1. Report by Eurostat, the official statistical reporting agency of the EU.
2. Forfás, *Comparative Consumer Prices in the Eurozone and Consumer Price Inflation in the Changeover period*, June 2002.
3. Data for 2006 World Competitiveness Yearbook, 2006.
4. Central Statistics website: <http://www.cso.ie>.
5. For measuring short-term inflationary trends in the domestic economy – as distinct from making long-term international inflationary comparisons – the author adheres to the Consumer Price Index, which includes the impact of mortgage interest payments.
6. Central Statistics Office, Quarterly National Household Survey (QNHS), 1st Quarter 2007, May.
7. At the time of writing, the European Central Bank had implemented eight quarter point rises in its main refinancing facility – effecting a total rise of 2 percentage points for most mortgage holders.

8. See Chapter 7.
9. Housing, water, gas, electricity and other fuels.
10. OECD, *Economic Surveys Ireland*, Volume 2006/3.
11. Restricting the quality of an outlet for the purposes of hygiene and public interest is a different matter.
12. Massey, P. and Daly, D., *Competition and Regulation in Ireland*, 2003.
13. Fine Gael, meaning 'the tribe of the Gaels', is the second largest party in the state and is centre-right in orientation.
14. Downes, J., report in the *Irish Times*, 3 December 2005.
15. Brennock, M., report in the *Irish Times*, 26 September 2006.
16. Guiomard, C., *The Irish Disease*, 1995.
17. RGDATA, a retail group, claimed reform could lead to 'ghost towns' emerging in Ireland.
18. Coleman, M., report in the *Irish Times*, 16 March 2007.

CHAPTER 7 – THE ONLY WAY IS UP

1. George Lee, *The End of the Oil Era*, paper presented to the Dublin Economics Workshop in Kenmare, October 2007.
2. According to the 2006 Census of Population, the area under the local authority jurisdiction of Dublin City Council was home to 506,211 persons.
3. ESRI, *Ex Ante Evaluation of the Investment Priorities for the National Development Plan 2007–2013*, 2006.
4. O'Brien, T., report in the *Irish Times*, 17 August 2007.
5. Central Statistics Office, 2006 Census of Population.
6. At this point, the following needs mention. The population given for Berlin relates to the city limits, whereas the population given for Dublin relates to the county border. The author regards this as fair because, as acknowledged in both the National Spatial Strategy 2002 document and the National Development Plan 2007–2013 document, the economic reality makes Dublin a city much bigger than its city limits would imply.
7. Central Statistics Office, 2006 Census of Population.

8. Central Statistics Office, 2006 Census of Population.

9. Indecon International Economic Consultants (prepared for the Western Development Commission), *Blueprint for Success: A Development Plan for the West*, 1999.

10. The study covered Donegal, Leitrim, Roscommon, Sligo, Mayo, Galway and Clare.

11. Germany's much vaunted economic problems have more to do with the high burden of taxation and government spending, beneath which lies a remarkably productive economy. In many respects Ireland is the opposite, hiding a lack of indigenous competitiveness beneath a tax regime that, compared to the EU average, is relatively low.

12. See <http://www.communities.gov.uk/documents/housing/xls/141389>. In January 2007, the weighted averaged valuation per hectare of land in London was STG £9,634,586 or €14,145,761.

13. McGreevy, R., report in the *Irish Times*, 4 September 2007.

14. Galway and Waterford do not have significant suburban populations and are treated by the Central Statistics Office as being self-contained city areas.

CHAPTER 8 – SHANNON VERSUS SHENZHEN

1. See Chapter 14.

2. The rule was to be phased out over an eighteen-month period, beginning in November 2006.

3. Tony Ryan passed away in October 2007, in the week of the book's completion.

4. Garret FitzGerald was an Aer Lingus executive in the 1950s.

5. See Shenzhen government online: <http://www.english.sz.gov.cn>.

6. Having said that, at 76.7 years the average life expectancy in the region is very respectable by European standards.

7. Although local labour market conditions were likely to have also played a role, as did a very favourable arrangement regarding airport charges between Shannon Airport and Aer Lingus' rival, Ryanair.

8. This is a conservative estimate of Belfast's attractiveness in this context. Whereas Shannon was competing for significant short

haul flights with Cork and Dublin, Belfast was the only major airport for the population of most of Ulster, i.e. around two million people.

9. Comprising counties Clare, Limerick and North Tipperary.
10. Central Statistics Office, 2006 Census of Population.
11. Limerick, Shannon, Tralee, Killarney and Ennis.
12. Brennan, C., report in the *Irish Times*, 20 August 2007.

CHAPTER 9 – PLANES, TRAINS AND AUTOMOBILES

1. Whelan, C., Fahy, T. and Russell, H., *'Best of Times? The Social Impact of the Celtic Tiger'*, ESRI, July 2007.
2. Where 'NDP' is used in the text, it refers specifically to the 2007–2013 programme, unless stated otherwise.
3. The four-year period during which the Luas line – the line in question – was opened for use.
4. Figures supplied by Tom O'Reilly of the Railway Procurement Agency.
5. ESRI, *Ex Ante Evaluation of the Investment Priorities for the National Development Plan 2007–2013*, 2006.
6. In 1834, fourteen years before the famine, Dargan built Ireland's first and one of Europe's first railway lines between Dún Laoghaire and Dublin City, a line still in use today.
7. Dublin Area Rapid Transport: a relatively efficient system of suburban rail running along Dublin's coast.
8. House prices in Dublin rose by 372 per cent between October 1996 and October 2006, compared to a 257 per cent rise outside Dublin. Dublin's attraction also pushed up house prices in its commuter belt (these rose by 294 per cent in the period), but this was due in large part to the relative underperformance of other cities in terms of job creation, a symptom of the 'Leinsterisation' of Ireland.
9. McCarthy, N., Fitzgerald, J. and Morgenroth, E., 'Transport Infrastructure', in *Ex-Ante Evaluation of the Investment Priorities For the National Development Plan 2007–2013*, ESRI, 2006.

Chapter 10 – The Legacy of Land

1. Dooley, T. The Land for the People, 2004.
2. This was revised.
3. Comptroller and Auditor General, Special Report for the Department of Transport, *National Roads Authority Primary Routes Improvement Programme*, April 2004.
4. O'Keeffe, Alan, report in the *Irish Independent*, 6 August 2007.
5. Department of Finance, Budgetary and Economic Statistics, 2007.
6. McDonald F., report in the *Irish Times*, 23 July 2007.
7. O'Regan, M., report in the *Irish Times*, 5 July 2006.
8. O'Brien, C., report in the *Irish Times*, 12 May 2006.
9. Speech by Minister Éamon Ó Cuív to an IRDA conference.
10. Central Statistics Office, 2006 Census of Population; Quarterly National Household Survey, September 2007.
11. Seanad debate on Sustainable Rural Housing Guidelines, 28 April 2005.
12. Irish Times, 8 April 2002.
13. Debate of Dáil Éireann's joint Committee on Agriculture and Food, 23 September 2003.
14. Seanad Debate on Sustainable Rural Housing Guidelines, 28 April 2005.
15. Following the election of June 2007, Dick Roche was appointed as a minister of state for European Affairs.

Chapter 11 – Ireland of the Hundred Governments

1. Sinn Féin, meaning 'we ourselves' is the oldest political party in the state and most strongly advocates national re-unification as well as having a left-of-centre economic platform.
2. If the government is unpopular, the minority's cause can become popular with the public causing 'ideological voters' to switch their voting patterns.
3. This tax was introduced in 1990 and required all residents of a local authority area to pay a lump sum to their council for the

provision of local services, regardless of how many of those services they used.

4. Gilbert, Martin, *Israel: A History*, 1998.
5. Including this author, who has not exercised it.
6. At the time of writing, Fianna Fáil is considering becoming active in Northern Ireland.
7. Socialist Party TD Joe Higgins, for example. Higgins lost his seat in the general election of June 2007.
8. Dublin, Fingal, Dún Laoghaire-Rathdown and South Dublin.
9. The eight regional authories are: Border (Donegal, Sligo, Leitrim, Cavan, Monaghan and Louth); Dublin (Dublin City and County); Midlands (Longford, Westmeath, Offaly and Laois); Mid-West (Clare, Limerick and Tipperary North Riding); South East (Carlow, Kilkenny, Tipperary South Riding, Wexford and Waterford); South West (Kerry and Cork); and West (Mayo, Roscommon and Galway).

Chapter 12 – A Nation Once Again

1. Northern Ireland Census 2002.
2. Impression gained by the author from a visit to Northern Ireland in July 2005.
3. Department of Finance, Budgetary and Economic Statistics, 2007.
4. By then elevated to the title of Lord Kilclooney.
5. Oliver, E., report in the *Irish Times*, 22 September 2006.
6. See Chapter 5.
7. Coleman, M., report in the *Irish Times*, 25 February 2006.
8. Report of Principal Outcomes of the Industrial Task Force, 2005.
9. November 2007.
10. McCaffrey, U., report in the *Irish Times*, 5 October 2007.

Chapter 13 – Once Again a Nation

1. O'Cathaoir, B., *The Famine Diary*, 1999.
2. See Chapter 2. 'Mourir' means 'to die'.

3. Donnelly, K., report in the *Irish Independent*, September 2007.
4. National Virtual Translation Centre (of the Foundation for Endangered Languages), see <http://www.nvtc.gov>.
5. Central Statistics Office, 2006 Census of Population, Volume 9.
6. Central Statistics Office, 2006 Census of Population.
7. See Chapter 10.
8. Chaplin's in Dublin's Hawkins Street being one example.
9. National Virtual Translation Centre (of the Foundation for Endangered Languages), see <http://www.nvtc.gov/lotw/months/august/Hebrew.html>.
10. Newspaper reports of the incident did not report the man's name.
11. O'Brien, B., report in the *Irish Times*, 25 August 2007.
12. Waters, John, report in the *Irish Times*, 26 June 2007.
13. See Fine Gael website: <http://www.finegael.ie>.
14. Dingle is the English language name of the town.

CHAPTER 14 – THE CURSE OF CLASS

1. Bord Fáilte is Ireland's official tourist board.
2. 'The Flight of the Earls' refers to the departure from Ireland on 14 September 1607 of two of Ulster's dominant chieftains, Hugh O'Neill, Earl of Tyrone, and Rory O'Donnell, Earl of Tyrconnell.
3. *The Irish Disease*, 1995.
4. A sociological study of growing alienation in the US.
5. Breen, R. and Whelan, C., *Social Mobility and Social Class in Ireland*, 1996.
6. In Tovey, H., *A Sociology of Ireland*, 2003.
7. Combat Poverty Agency press release, 4 September 2007.
8. Combat Poverty Agency, Watson, D., Whelan, C.T., Williams, J. and Blackwell, S., *Mapping Poverty National Regional and County Patterns*, 2005.

CHAPTER 15 – 1607–2007: THE RETURN OF THE EARLS

1. Central Statistics Office, 2006 Census of Population.

2. Barrett A., McCarthy, Y., *The Earnings of Immigrants in Ireland*: *Results from the 2005 EU Survey of Income and Living Conditions*, ESRI working paper no. 206, August 2007.
3. Gurdgiev, C., *Migration and EU Enlargement*, a paper for Danish think tank CEPOS, March 2006.
4. Gilbert, Martin, *Israel: A History*, 1998.
5. 17 September 2007.

APPENDIX – 1707–2007: SCOTLAND'S CHOICE

1. *Let Scotland Flourish*, Scottish National Party document, 2006.

Bibliography

Akenson, D.H., *The Irish Diaspora*: *A Primer*, Toronto: P.D. Meany, 1993.

Baldwin, R. and Wyplosz, C., *The Economics of European Integration*, UK: McGraw-Hill Higher Education.

Breen, R. and Whelan, C., *Social Mobility and Social Class in Ireland*, Dublin: Gill and Macmillan, 1996.

Combat Poverty Agency, Watson, D., Whelan, C.T., Williams, J. and Blackwell, S., *Mapping Poverty*: *National Regional and County Patterns*, Dublin: ESRI, 2005.

Dooley, T., *The Land for the People: The Land Question in Independent Ireland*, Dublin: University College Dublin Press, 2004.

Foster, R.F., *Modern Ireland*, 1600–1972, London: Penguin Books, 1990.

Gallup, J.L., Sachs, D.J. and Mellinger, A.D., *Geography and Economic Development*, NBER Working Paper 6849, December 1998.

Gilbert, Martin, *Israel: A History*, London: Black Swan, 1998.

Guiomard, C., *The Irish Disease and How to Cure it*: *Common Sense Economics for a Professional World*, Dublin: Oak Tree Press, 1995.

Hatton, T. and Williamson, J., *The Age of Mass Migration*: *Causes and Impact*, USA: Oxford University Press, 1998.

O'Cathaoir, B, *The Famine Diary*, Dublin: Irish Academic Press, 1999.

O'Grada, C., *Ireland's Great Famine*: *Interdisciplinary Perspectives*, Dublin: University College Dublin Press, 2006.

O'Hagan, J., *The Economy of Ireland*: *Policy and Performance of a Small European Country*, Basingstoke: Palgrave MacMillan, 2004.

Poirteir, C., *The Great Irish Famine*, Cork: Mercier Press, 1995.

Putnam, Robert, *Bowling Alone*: *The Collapse and Revival of American Community*, US: Simon & Schuster, 2001.

Mankiw, G., Romer, D. and Weil, D., 'A Contribution to the Empirics of Economic Growth', *Quarterly Journal of Economics*, 107, 1992, pp. 407–437.

Massey, P. and Daly, D., *Competition and Regulation in Ireland: The Law and Economics*, Dublin: Oak Tree Press, 2003.

Riain, S., *The Politics of High Tech Growth: Developmental Network States in the Global Economy*, Cambridge: Cambridge University Press, 2004.

Swift, J., *A Modest Proposal*, pamphlet originally published in 1729, in *A Modest Proposal and Other Satires*, UK: Prometheus Books, 1995.

Whelan, C., Fahy, T. and Russell, H., *Best of Times? The Social Impact of the Celtic Tiger*, Dublin: ESRI, July 2007.

Index